I Have a Question About God...

Doctrine for Children...
and Their Parents!

I Have a Question About God...

Doctrine for Children...
and Their Parents!

Cheryl Fawcett
Robert C. Newman

ILLUSTRATIONS BY RON MAZELLAN

Regular Baptist Press
1300 North Meacham Road
Schaumburg, Illinois 60173-4888

I HAVE A QUESTION ABOUT GOD
© 1994 Regular Baptist Press
Schaumburg, Illinois

All Scripture references are from the King James Version unless otherwise noted.

Library of Congress Cataloging-in-Publication Data
Fawcett, Cheryl, 1953–
    I have a question about God: doctrine for children and their parents / Cheryl Fawcett
and Robert C. Newman.
        p. cm.
ISBN 0-87227-180-3
        1. Theology, Doctrinal—Popular works—Juvenile literature. 2. Baptists—
Doctrines—Juvenile literature. [1. Theology. 2. Baptists. 3. Christian life.]
I. Newman, Robert C., 1936– .
II. Title
BT77.F368   1994   94-3054
248.8'45—dc20   CIP AC

To
my nieces and nephews
Melissa, Monica, Amanda,
Erin, Matthew, Carrie and Andrew,
who keep me sharp by asking
important questions about God
—Cheryl Fawcett

To
Barbara
Charles
Donna
Roberta
—Robert C. Newman

Contents

Preface

We are happy to have the task of completing this book behind us. We present it to our readers with a profound sense of God's direction.

The book's purpose is to close a gap in the hearts and minds of young children concerning the Bible and its teaching. Years spent teaching children, youth and adults have driven us to the reality that most of us know the Biblical story but not its message. Therefore, this teaching tool creates a simple way of getting beyond the Biblical text and toward a practical knowledge of its message.

We want to thank Regular Baptist Press and Dr. Vernon D. Miller, executive editor, and Mr. Norman Olson, book editor, for their willingness to publish the book.

We thank Mr. Joe Ragont for providing his expertise in the area of graphics.

We express our gratitude to my wife, Betty, for her patience in keeping us at it. She also has proved to be a practical resource person.

Introduction

Adult Friend,

My name is Bob! And I'm Cheryl! We love children and have worked with them for a long time. We have written this book for them—and for you.

Kids ask tough questions. Every little child is a budding theologian. We want to help you answer their tough questions. Young children have tender and inquisitive minds. We want to help you give them true, satisfying and simple answers from the Bible. For example, has your child asked you, "Mom, Dad, where did I come from?" This question from a young child tends to be more theological than biological. By the time children reach junior high, the question will probably be more biological than theological. But for now, you must provide simple, straightforward answers that will encourage their faith. Simple as these questions seem, the answers you provide must be true and Biblical if they are to last a lifetime.

We will begin each section with hints for you in understanding what the Bible says about that doctrine. Then we will provide a story in which a child asks an important question.

In former times, theologians wrote and used catechisms to instruct the young children. These question-and-answer manuals helped them understand the Lord's Prayer, the Apostles' Creed and the Ten Commandments. In these modern times, however, we have more access to helping children understand the meaning behind the information. While the basic information is still necessary, we must aid children in applying the truth to their everyday living. Our narratives will attempt to do just that: ask a question, provide a Biblical answer, and encourage Biblical living.

This book is a tool to help you understand and get more out of the Bible. Our purpose is to set you loose reading and loving the Bible for yourself. Therefore, may we suggest that you read aloud the context (the chapter around the section's high-lighted verse) before you teach your child. While he or she may not understand every word, the practice of reading the Bible together will prove useful as a pattern later.

1
I Have a Question About GOD

Hints and Helps

Keep it simple! Take, for example, Genesis 1:1: "In the beginning God created the heaven and the earth." This statement is profound yet simple. To the scientist and the young child alike, the Bible says one thing. God is before all that we know and see, and He made all that we know and see. The Scriptures do not debate God; they affirm Him without question. He is! He does! Most important is for us to call children to faith, not provide them with a detailed explanation.

Verse to Memorize

Jonah 4:2c: "I know that You are a gracious and merciful God, slow to anger, and abundant in lovingkindness, One who relents from doing harm" (NKJV).

Who Is God?

Hi! My name is Topher. Really my name is Christopher, but my friends call me Toph or Topher. I'm eight. I like to ride my bike and play T-ball, soccer and basketball.

I have two sisters, Megan and Bobbie. Megan is ten and plays the piano— all the time. She takes lessons. Roberta is four. We call her Bobbie. She's fun to tease. But she drives me nuts, always asking "What's that?" or "What does this mean?" Mom and Dad say she'll grow out of always asking questions, but I doubt it.

She did it just yesterday. In the afternoon a man came to our house. Bobbie ran to the door, and right after Mom opened it, she asked, "Who are you?"

"Bobbie," Mom said.

But the man smiled. "I'm a fireman. I help people when they are sick and need to get to the hospital or when they have a crash in their car or when their house catches on fire. Right now I'm collecting money for the fire department."

The fireman talked to Mom for a while. I think she even gave him some money. When he left, Bobbie asked right away, "What is a fireman like?"

"He told you he helps people, Bobbie," I had to remind her.

"But what is he like?" Bobbie asked the same question again.

Mom answered that time. "He is helpful and hardworking. He is a fine neighbor."

"Is God like that too? Would He be a good neighbor?"

Mom was quiet for a minute. I could tell she was thinking. "No one has ever asked me that before, Bobbie," she finally said. "I'm not sure how to answer you. When I was a little girl, I went to church and read the Bible a lot, but it's been a long time. Let me think . . . God is holy."

"What does 'holy' mean?" When Mom answers one question, Bobbie always asks another one. See why I go crazy?

She told Bobbie, " 'Holy' means that God is set apart from sin. We can think of sin as being dirty and holy as being clean. I remember, too, that angels called out that God is holy, holy, holy."

"That means God is really, really, really clean. Does He take a lot of baths?"

"No, it means He does what is right."

"How does He know what is right?"

"He is God, and whatever He does is right. He knows everything too, so He knows everything that is right and wrong."

I asked Mom, "You mean God never does anything wrong?"

"No, never."

Bobbie said, "I wish I was God so I would never do anything wrong."

I laughed. "Bobbie, you can't be God."

Mom told us, "You both can be like Him. He wants you to do what is right all the time."

16

"Does God love me?"
"Yes, He does, Bobbie."
"Does He love Toph?"
"God loves everyone!"
"Even Michael Lobatosky?"
"Yes, even Michael."
"Does He love Mikki, our cat?"

"Yes, God loves all the creatures. He made them, you know."

"I think God would be a good neighbor."

"Yes, Bobbie, I think He would be the best neighbor you could ever have."

Verses to Read

John 3:16: "For God so loved the world that He gave His only begotten Son, that whoever believes in Him should not perish but have everlasting life" (NKJV).

Leviticus 11:44: "I am the LORD your God; consecrate yourselves and be holy, because I am holy" (NIV).

Genesis 1:1: "In the beginning God created the heaven and the earth."

QUESTIONS TO ASK YOUR CHILD
1. What is God like?
2. What does "holy" mean?
3. How can you be holy?

Where Does God Live?

On the first day of school, Megan was dressed and ready early. She always is. Mom had to help Bobbie put on the new clothes we had bought the week before at some big department store. I was supposed to be brushing my teeth, but I got to playing with some toys in the bathroom sink.

Then Mom called, "Hurry now, everyone, or you'll be late!" She gave each of us a kiss at the front door. We practically ran to the corner and waited for the school bus. When it came, we jumped on and found seats. Megan and

Bobbie sat right behind the bus driver; I sat behind them with my friend, Tommy.

Megan started asking Bobbie questions about her address and phone number. See, it was Bobbie's first day at preschool, and she needed to know that stuff. "Where do you live, Bobbie?" Megan asked.

"In that big blue house."

"No, I mean what is your house number and street name?"

"Ummm . . . 1022 Brewster Courthouse."

"It's just Court, Bobbie, not courthouse," I told her. "The courthouse is downtown."

"Oh yeah, you're right."

"What's your town?" Megan continued.

"It's the one after we go through the big bridge over the river."

"What is its name, silly?" I think Megan was getting a little impatient.

"It's Grafton. Mom told you not to call me silly," Bobbie told her. Then Bobbie looked out the window and was actually quiet for a few seconds before she asked, "Megan, where does God live?"

"I don't know. Let's ask the bus driver." We were at a stoplight, so Meagan tapped the bus driver on the shoulder. He's a nice man. He's driven my school bus two years. "Mr. Bus Driver, where does God live?" Megan asked him. I couldn't hear his answer. When Megan sat back down, I asked her what he said.

"He doesn't know either. He said we should ask our mom and dad."

Bobbie had a good first day at school. She remembered our house number and street name and even the name of our town without any help. And she remembered her question too. When Mom picked her up from preschool, the first thing she said was, "Where does God live?"

Mom told her, "He lives very far away."

"You mean like by Grandma and Grandpa? They live really, really far away."

"Farther than that," Mom tried to explain. "He lives out of this world."

"Like Star Wars!"

"No, Bobbie, Star Wars is pretend. God lives in a real place. He lives in a place the Bible calls Heaven. But it's so far away that no person has ever been there."

"Is it a pretend, make-believe place?" I think Bobbie was confused. Actually I was kind of confused too.

Mom found her Bible and looked in the back part under the word "Heaven." She found a place and read to us. " 'For God is in heaven, and you on earth; therefore let your words be few.' Ecclesiastes 5:2. There it is. God is in Heaven, and you are on earth. It's like a song I learned when I was your age. 'Heaven is a wonderful place, Filled with glory and grace, I want to see my Savior's face. Heaven is a wonderful, Heaven is a glorious, Heaven is a wonderful place.' "

QUESTIONS TO ASK YOUR CHILD

1. Where does the Bible say God lives?
2. Can you see Heaven? Why not?
3. Since Heaven is so far away, how can you believe God lives there?

Does God Have a Wife?

My dad's great! He's a carpenter, so he works with wood and nails and ladders and saws and stuff like that. Sometimes he takes me to see the houses he builds. That's the greatest!

One time last summer, Mom and Megan were going to Eastman to buy a new book for piano lessons. I don't like shopping very much, so I asked to go with Dad. Of course, when Bobbie heard me ask, she wanted to go too.

When we got to the place, I saw a big woodpile and a huge hole in the ground. Dad's workers had put concrete into the ground to make "footers." I think that's what Dad said.

We met Dad's helpers, John and Kirby. I saw Kirby lift six boards by himself! Bobbie and I moved one board a little ways. Then Dad told us to play on a pile of sand while he, John and Kirby put in the floorboards or something.

Bobbie's not bad—for a girl. She likes to play with trucks, and she doesn't

care if she gets dirty. I had three trucks, and we made lots of roads in the sand. We had fun until lunch.

I had taken only one bite of my sandwich when Bobbie started asking crazy questions again. "John, do you have a mother?"

"She meant, 'Do you have a wife?' I think." I had to help, since Bobbie doesn't always say the right words.

"Yeah, do you have a wife?" Bobbie asked.

"I sure do." John was smiling. "She's beautiful and kind, and she loves me a lot."

Then Bobbie asked, "Kirby, do you have a mother? I mean—wife?" Kirby didn't say anything. He just looked . . . kind of red. Bobbie must have asked the wrong question again.

"He's working on it," John said, "but the girl doesn't know it yet. Actually, she does act more like his mother sometimes. That's probably why he's turning all red."

"I am not red! But I do have a great girlfriend. I like her a lot. We're getting to know each other better. I hope someday she'll be my wife."

Then Kirby smiled funny at my dad and asked him, "Gary, how about you? Do you have a wife, or 'mother,' as Bobbie likes to say?" I thought that was the silliest question.

But Dad smiled and said, "I do indeed. She's the best woman I've ever known. I don't know what I'd do without her."

"Dad, does God have a wife?" Bobbie said the right word, but what a question!

"I mean, what would God do without a wife like Mom?"

"Well, actually, God is perfect in Himself."

Then Bobbie wanted to know, "What does 'perfect' mean?"

"It means God doesn't need anyone or anything to make Him better. He doesn't need anyone to help Him."

Dad stopped—I think he was thinking. Then he said, "In the Bible God does call Himself a father. When we think of God in that way, we earth people can understand a little better what He is like."

"But will God ever find a wife?" Bobbie looked kind of worried.

"Actually, Muffin"—I don't know why Dad calls her that—"God doesn't need to find a wife. There's no one on earth or in Heaven who is like Him. He is satisfied just like He is."

"God will get lonely without a wife."

Dad smiled again. "No, He won't. God is happy by Himself. He knows that people get lonely though—just like Adam did. God made a helper who was perfect for Adam. She helped keep him company and was the mother of his children. God allows us to have mothers and fathers and be children in families. But God does not have a wife."

"God has a Son."

"You're right, Bobbie. And we'll talk about that more when we get home tonight. Now you build roads with Toph, while I finish this house floor."

"OK." Bobbie grabbed the little red truck before she asked me, "Toph, did you know God doesn't need a wife?"

QUESTIONS TO ASK YOUR CHILD

1. Why doesn't God need anyone to help Him?
2. Do you ever need a helper? Why?

Does God Have
Any Children?

I guess Megan and Mom had a good trip to Eastman. They found the music book they wanted, and Megan said she tried out new pianos. I'm glad I wasn't there. Megan also said they ate lunch at Burger World. Mom brought me and Bobbie the meal-box toys. They were these little plastic people things.

Bobbie put her toy girl on the table at dinnertime. "Toph, where's your little boy?"

"I left him in my room." I was thinking about something else. "Mom, you know that new Carter family down the street? How many kids do they have?"

"They have four children."

"That's what I thought, but yesterday I saw six kids playing in the backyard. They told me they all live there."

"Oh, the Carters have two foster children." Dad passed me the hamburger hot dish.

"What are foster children?"

"They're children who have had trouble in their own family and need someplace to stay for a while."

"But are Mr. and Mrs. Carter their mom and dad?"

"Well, the Carters are acting as their mom and dad."

"Forever?"

"Well, that depends on what happens with their own mom and dad. If they work out their problems with money and jobs, the kids may get to live with them again. But the children's real dad is also in trouble with the police. The government people won't let the children go back unless he gets help."

"What if their dad doesn't get help? Who will be their family then?" Dad said the Carters might adopt the kids if their parents didn't get help.

"What does 'adopt' mean?" Bobbie asked that.

"It means to choose children to be part of your family."

"Mom, does God have a son?"

"The Bible calls Jesus God's Son. But it's not exactly like human fathers and sons. Have you heard John 3:16? 'For God so loved the world, that He gave His only begotten Son, that whosoever believeth in Him should not perish, but have everlasting life.' " Of course, Megan said she knew that whole thing.

"Mom, does God have any girls?"

"No, He has only one Son, Jesus," Mom said.

"Maybe God could adopt a girl. Maybe He could adopt lots of girls."

Mom had her Bible open, and I could tell she was going to read something.

"Here's the verse. John 1:12. It does talk about people becoming God's children—boys and girls. 'But as many as received Him, to them He gave the right to become children of God.' God is a father to people who trust Jesus as Savior."

"Forever?" Bobbie asked.

"Yes, forever. Just like the Carters, God will keep loving His adopted children. He may correct us, but we will always be His children once we believe on Him."

"Mom, did God adopt you?"

"Yes, Bobbie, when I was a little girl. I would like you to think about being adopted into God's family too."

QUESTIONS TO ASK YOUR CHILD

1. Who is God's Son?
2. How can you be adopted into God's family?
3. Once you have been adopted into God's family, will you always belong to His family?

How Old Is God?

The Schmidts' neighbor Mrs. Greene is really old. She needs lots of help, so Mom is always taking Bobbie and Megan to see her and do stuff for her.

Mrs. Greene lives in a really old house. The sidewalk is all broken and crooked. The shutters on the windows are about to fall off. The mailbox is rusted. Weeds are everywhere. Mom said that Mrs. Greene's house used to be the prettiest one on the street.

Mrs. Greene can't walk too well anymore, so she uses a walker to help her move without falling. Whenever Bobbie rings the doorbell, it takes Mrs. Green a long time to answer the door.

Bobbie usually finds some flowers and takes them to Mrs. Greene to cheer her up.

Not too long ago, it was Mrs. Greene's birthday. Bobbie took flowers like usual. And Megan had helped Mom bake a small cake and decorate it. They took that too.

Bobbie rang the doorbell. Mrs. Greene's doorbell makes a really loud DING DONG! While they waited, Bobbie, Megan and Mom decided to sing to Mrs. Greene when she got to the door.

"Happy birthday to you! Happy birthday to you! Happy birthday, Mrs. Greene! Happy birthday to you!"

"How old are you anyway?" Bobbie and her questions did it again!

"It's not polite to ask a lady her age, Bobbie." Mom said that quickly before Mrs. Greene could catch her breath and answer.

"Are you 200?" Bobbie doesn't know when to stop asking questions.

"Bobbie, please apologize to Mrs. Greene," Mom told her.

"I'm sorry." Bobbie looked at her shoes. She does that when she feels bad.

"That's OK, honey. I'm old, but not that old yet. Actually this is my 83rd birthday. I just feel like 200 some days."

Mrs. Greene liked her cake and flowers. Mom, Bobbie and Megan had a little party with her. Then on the way home, Bobbie started asking questions again. "Mom, how old are you?"

"As old as my tongue and a little older than my teeth," answered Mom.

"How old is Dad?"

"Oh, much older than I am," Mom said. Mom was teasing. At least, she was smiling.

"How old is Mikki, our cat?"

"In people years she's about 60."

"How old is God?"

"Too old to count."

"Why?"

Mom answered her. "Well, the Bible says that before God made the world,

He was there. The Bible uses the word 'eternal' to describe Him."

"What's 'eternal' mean?"

"It means without beginning or ending. God never had a birthday."

"You mean He never gets a birthday cake? How does He remember how old He is? Is God too old to walk, like Mrs. Greene?"

"God is different from people. We are born. We count our years one at a time, and we die. God always was and always will be. We can't count His years, because they never started and will never end. God doesn't have a body like you and I do. He is perfect. He never gets old or worn out."

Then Megan said, "It's like God is forever young and never old."

"Something like that, honey."

Verses to Read

Deuteronomy 33:27: "The eternal God is your refuge, And underneath are the everlasting arms . . . " (NKJV).

Psalm 90:2: "Before the mountains were brought forth, Or ever You had formed the earth and the world, Even from everlasting to everlasting, You are God" (NKJV).

QUESTIONS TO ASK YOUR CHILD

1. Does God have a birthday? Why not?
2. What does "eternal" mean?

Does God Get Tired, Hungry or Sleepy?

The night before we went to Grandma and Grandpa's house, I couldn't wait for morning! I kept looking at my alarm clock all night long, wishing it would say 6:00. We live in Ohio, and it takes us a long time to get to where they live.

All our suitcases were ready. We only had to put on our clothes, eat some cereal and brush our teeth. Megan helped Dad with the suitcases. Bobbie was getting some books to read on the way—well, actually for me to read to her. I helped Mom get finished up in the kitchen. We were ready to go.

All morning we just looked out the car windows. The corn was growing. And we saw lots of cows in the fields. We played the license plate game for a while. I won! We stopped at a rest area and ate a picnic lunch that Mom had packed. Bobbie ran around and rolled in the grass. When we got back in the car, Bobbie asked me to read to her. I read all ten books—two times each.

But Bobbie was still not happy. She kept wiggling. Mom says we're "restless" when we're like that. Then Bobbie began to cry. "Are we almost there? I'm tired. I'm hungry."

"Take a little nap, and we'll be there soon," Mom told her.

"I can't; there's no room back here. I'm tired, Mom. I'm hungry."

Mom had some snacks packed in the trunk, so Dad stopped at the next rest stop and got them out. Pretzels and apples helped a little. Mom got out a surprise book for Bobbie to color too.

Bobbie colored for a while, but we still had a long way to go before we would get to Grandpa and Grandma's.

"I'm tired! I'm hungry! Aren't we there yet?"

"No, not yet. But we are much closer, Bobbie."

Bobbie put her head on Megan's lap for a second. Then she sat up again. "Mom, does God ever get tired and hungry? Does God ever sleep?"

Mom had been reading her Bible to help pass the time, and I guess she was at a good place to answer Bobbie. "Listen as I read a verse to you from the Bible. 'My help comes from the LORD, Who made heaven and earth. . . . He who keeps you will not slumber. Behold, He who keeps Israel—' "

"What's Israel?"

"Israel is a nation that God chose as His special people. God watches over them in extra special ways. 'He who keeps Israel shall neither slumber nor sleep.'"

"What's 'slumber'?"

" 'Slumber' is another way to say 'sleep.' "

"Would God sleep if He had to ride in the car a long time?"

"Well, Bobbie, God doesn't need to travel anywhere because He is everywhere at the same time."

I wish I could be everywhere. It must be great being God. He never gets tired or hungry, and He never has to sit in a crowded backseat.

QUESTIONS TO ASK YOUR CHILD

1. Does God ever sleep?
2. Why doesn't God have to travel from one place to another?

Does God Get Sick or Die?

Grandpa had just left for the sheep barn, and I asked Mom if I could go. Bobbie wanted to go too. There were new lambs, and we wanted to see them. Mom said we could, so we ran to catch up with Grandpa. The barn doesn't have any rooms—just these high feeder bins for the ewes. Ewes are girl sheep, and rams are boys. Grandpa had one really big ram tied up in a corner of the barn behind a fence. "Rams tend to be mean," Grandpa warned us.

That ram looked mean too. I wasn't going to go near him! When Grandpa fed the ram, it tried to hit him with its horns. And it knocked over the pail of grain Grandpa was going to feed it. Grandpa did let me throw some hay to the ram, but I didn't go inside its fence. When Grandpa came out, I moved out of the way!

When we got done in the barn, we went to check on some ewes that were out in the field with their baby lambs. Grandpa had me carry a pail of water to give the sheep. One ewe had one lamb. Another ewe had twins, and another ewe had triplets. Grandpa said ewes don't usually have triplets. And one of the triplet lambs was sick. I could tell which one it was right away because it was really small and it laid very still. The other lambs were getting milk from their mothers, but the sick one couldn't even do that.

"Will that lamb die, Grandpa?" I wished Bobbie hadn't asked that.

"I don't know for sure, but in a few days we'll be able to tell better. I'll call the veterinarian this afternoon and ask her what I should do to help."

"I don't want the lamb to die, Grandpa. Is it very sick?"

"I think it'll probably be OK."

"Grandpa, does God get sick?"

Grandpa always tells us that he loves God, and he knows lots of stuff about God too. Grandpa can even answer Bobbie's really hard questions.

"That's a good question, Bobbie. Let's go back to the house, and I'll read to you from the Psalms. People and animals get sick. Sometimes our bodies don't work right. Sometimes we eat something that makes us sick. Sometimes we get sick from germs."

"I got the chicken pox from Toph."

"People get sick all the time," Grandpa said. "But God is a spirit. He is real, but He doesn't have a body like you and I do. He doesn't get sick. He doesn't catch cold or get the flu or chicken pox. His heart never gets tired or worn out. He never breaks a bone, because He has no bones."

"Why do we have to get sick then?" I wanted to know that. I had missed two T-ball games one time when I had the flu.

Grandpa started to answer. "When God made Adam, Adam was perfect. He would not get sick, and he would have lived forever. But Adam sinned. He disobeyed God. God had to punish Adam for eating the fruit God had told him

to leave alone. The Bible says that Adam and everyone after him would die because he disobeyed."

"That's a hard punishment!" I said.

I guess Bobbie was thinking the same thing. She asked, "Is God mean?"

"No, Bobbie, He's holy and just. He can't stand sin. But God did make a way for man to live forever with Him in Heaven through Jesus."

"My mom and dad tell me about Jesus," Bobbie said. "Does God ever die?

Who would take care of the world and hold it together and make rain and sunshine?"

"Don't worry, Bobbie. God will never die. He will always be able to take care of people and animals and the earth. The Bible says, 'But You, O LORD, shall endure forever. . . . Your years are throughout all generations. . . . You laid the foundation of the earth. . . . They will perish, but You will endure. . . . You are the same, and Your years will have no end' " (Psalm 102:12, 24–27; NKJV).

> ### QUESTIONS TO ASK YOUR CHILD
>
> 1. Will God ever get sick?
> 2. Will God ever die?
> 3. Why do you get sick?

How Do We Know About God?

We had to go to bed early, but that was OK. The next day we were going to the Hartford Fair! Grandpa told us about it at supper. "It's the granddaddy of all the fairs in our part of Pennsylvania. You can ride rides and see animals, beautiful flowers, crafts and woodworking. And the fair has lots of food and ice cream too!"

"Aunt Ginny and Uncle Bill always run the ice cream booth. They'll sell you a huge cone for only one dollar." Grandma smiled at me when she said that. She knows I like ice cream a lot. Megan got excited when Grandma told her about the music in the grandstand. Bobbie just wanted to see the sheep, goats, pigs, horses and cows. We all wanted to go with Grandma to see if her pickles and corn would win any prizes.

The fair was great! It seemed like Grandpa knew everybody there. He took Megan and me into the craft display. We looked at lots of pictures with stitching.

"I think this one must have taken forever." Megan was pointing at the biggest picture in the row.

"Well, not forever, but a long time. The lady who made it is willing to work a long time on something to do good work."

"How do you know, Grandpa?" It was Bobbie! I hadn't even noticed that she was following us until she started her questions.

"Well, child, notice how even her stitches are. Every one is perfectly in line with the others. Look at the beautiful colors she chose. People show a lot about themselves in the things they make. You can tell which ladies are careful—which ones take extra time. Look at this picture." He pointed to another picture.

"It's the same design." I said that.

"Who made that one, Grandpa? The colors are dull," Megan said.

"The tag on the frame says Mrs. Browne. I'm not surprised; she wears dull dresses too."

"Look at this blue ribbon, Grandpa!" I had gone down the row ahead of them. "Who d'ya think made this one?" I wanted Grandpa to guess.

"Why, that looks like your Grandma's work. I'd know it anywhere." Grandpa looked proud.

"You saw her doing it, didn't you, Grandpa?" Megan asked.

"No, I was outside with the sheep when she made this picture, but it is just like her. You can tell a person by his work, you know."

After we left the craft display, we rode rides and ate ice cream. Then we listened to music in the grandstands. Bobbie had to see all the animals and pet each one. I had so much fun I didn't want to leave, but the fair had to close down for the night.

Grandpa had to carry Bobbie to the car. I thought she was asleep until she asked, "Grandpa, how do you know so much about God? Did you see Him?"

"Well, not face-to-face, but I sure learn a lot by looking at all the beautiful things He made."

"What did God make, Grandpa?"

"See those beautiful hills over there? And the gorgeous stars? All those fruits and vegetables you saw today in the vegetable barn and at the 4-H

display are God's work. The flowers we saw today are God's handiwork. And see those thunderclouds over there?"

"A big storm is coming. Is God mad?"

"No, Bobbie, He's just watering the earth so more of our crops will grow. I've traveled many places, and everywhere I go I learn more about how great and awesome my God really is."

"You learn about God from seeing the world?"

"Some of what I know, but not all. Do you remember today when we looked at the tags on the pictures?"

"The tags told about the ladies who made the pictures." Megan reminded Bobbie about them.

"Yes, I remember," Bobbie said. "Does the earth have a tag on it, Grandpa?" Bobbie's eyes were closed. She asks funnier questions when she's tired.

"Well not actually a tag, but God gave us the Bible to tell us much more about Him than we could ever have guessed by just looking at the things He made. Creation tells us some things, but the Bible helps us understand a lot more about God. Some people get so excited about what God made that they never take time to read more about Him."

Grandpa put Bobbie into the car, and she finally opened her eyes. "I will be able to read by myself pretty soon. Do you have a Bible for me?"

"I'm so glad you asked that, little one."

Verses to Read
  Psalm 19:1–14

QUESTIONS TO ASK YOUR CHILD

1. What are two things that teach us about God?
2. By looking at what God has made, what do you think God is like?

2
I Have a Question About
CREATION

Hints and Helps

True science, true faith and the Scriptures complement each other; they do not contradict each other. The creation account, Genesis 1 and 2, tells the beautiful and true story about the one true, triune God Who created everything for man, whom He made in His image. The creation narrative pictures God creating a perfect, complete and ready-to-go world. Within this world God created a special home for the creatures He loves. As a parent you may have experienced this sense of creating a special place as you lovingly and carefully prepared your heart and home for your new child.

According to the Genesis account, God created everything and put it into place before the principal characters, Adam and Eve, arrived on the scene. God created natural elements for man, not man for the elements, or world. Adam was to manage the earth and care for it wisely.

This special place, the Garden of Eden, was the location for conversation and intimacy between the infinite, all-loving Creator and the finite, responding creatures, Adam and Eve.

Verses to Memorize

Genesis 1:1: "In the beginning God created the heaven and the earth."

Genesis 1:27: "So God created man in His own image; in the image of God He created him; male and female He created them" (NKJV).

Where Did Stars Come From?

Tent. Shovel. Compass. Map. Fishing pole. Reel. Paddles. Canoe. Lifejackets. Food. Dad and I made a final check before we left for the High Sky Country Camping Grounds. We had talked about this camping trip forever. I even had a dream about fishing. Finally it was the day!

As soon as it was light out, Dad and I got in the car. We headed for the mountains. It was just Dad and me and the outdoors—it was going to be great! I had saved my allowance since Christmas and had enough money to buy an army knife. It had everything!

We got to the camp in the afternoon and set up our campsite. We even had time to take a boat ride and go fishing on old Canuge Lake before dinner. I caught a big fish. Well, it was big for me—five inches long. Anyway it was long enough to keep, and I used my new knife to help Dad scale it. The fish tasted so good. We roasted marshmallows and made "somemores" for our bedtime snack.

As it got darker, I started hearing all the noises in the woods. I could hear bird noises, dog noises, other-people noises and howling noises. I even heard a harmonica! I wasn't going to be afraid. I just asked Dad if the noises were outdoor kinds of noises. When I had to go to the bathroom across the camping area, I asked Dad to go with me because it was really dark.

"Wow, Dad, look at all those stars! We don't have that many stars where we live."

"Well, actually we do, son."

"No, we don't. I've looked before, and we only have a few stars in our town."

"No, son, the city lights hide the stars from your view. Actually these are the same stars, but you can see them better because it's so dark here."

"Where did stars come from, Dad? I heard someone say that a big planet exploded and made a bunch of them."

"Some people believe that, but it's not what really happened. The Bible says that God made the stars."

"Does the Bible tell how God did it?" I thought maybe God had a star machine or something.

"No, son, the Bible just says that He did it."

"Why did He make them?"

Dad looked up at the sky before he said anything. "We have them to give light to the earth so we can see a little at night."

"But how come they aren't as bright as the sun?"

"God wanted us to have day and night, so He made some lights bigger and stronger than others."

I wished God had made them a little brighter. I asked Dad how many stars there are.

Even though it was dark, I could see Dad smile. "Why don't you try to count them?"

"OK. One, two, three, four, uhh . . . one, two, three, four . . ."

"What's wrong?"

"Every time I start, I get mixed up and have to start over. There are so many I probably couldn't count that high."

Dad messed up my hair like he does sometimes. "I couldn't count that high either. What does that tell you about God?"

"Well, He must be really strong and powerful to make so many stars. And He must be perfect to know where to put them all."

Verses to Read
    Job 9:9; Psalm 147:9; Genesis 22:17; Genesis 26:4

You may want to take your child to a planetarium to explore the vast expanse of the stars.

QUESTIONS TO ASK YOUR CHILD

1. How were the stars made?
2. Why do we have the stars?
3. Can you count all the stars in the sky?

Who Made Dirt?

Megan is a typical girl. She wants everything to be perfectly clean all the time. But I love dirt and getting dirty and staying dirty. While we visited Grandma and Grandpa's farm, I got really dirty every day. One time I played in the barn with the sheep and lambs. Then I threw the softball against the barn wall. I climbed trees. I helped Grandpa pull weeds and pick peas in the garden. I got to ride on the tractor and help Grandpa plow the fields. It was great!

Grandpa likes getting dirty too. His old overalls are super dirty! I think he's

been working on getting them good and dirty for a long time. Grandma won't let him wear them in the house. He has to take them off and hang them in the shed after he does the chores. Then he can go in the house for dinner.

Megan didn't go outside much at the farm. She stayed inside and helped Grandma in the kitchen. They baked cookies and pies and homemade bread. They fixed us a huge dinner every lunchtime.

Sometimes I'd leave Grandpa, and I'd go inside to see what Grandma and Megan were doing. Every time I went in, Megan yelled at me, "Topher, stop tracking mud into the kitchen!" I wiped my shoes at the door. Sometimes I even took off my shoes and left them on the porch. Once, though, I forgot and got big globs of black dirt on the floor and all across the dining room. Boy, was Megan mad! She got the broom and started chasing me out of the house.

Bobbie was sitting in Grandma's big chair, coloring in her new book. She kept coloring when she asked, "Who made dirt anyway, Grandma? It's terrible stuff, don't you think?"

"Well, it all depends on the kind of dirt you're talking about and where it is."

"What d'ya mean?" Bobbie did stop coloring.

"God made dirt. The Bible says so," Grandma started to explain.

I guess Megan found that hard to believe. She asked, "Grandma, where does it say that?"

"Genesis 1, verses 9 and 10, tell us, 'Then God said, . . . let the dry land appear: and it was so. And God called the dry land Earth. . . . And God saw that it was good.' "

"Dirt can't be good. It makes a mess on the floor and on people's clothes and shoes." Megan really doesn't like dirt.

"The next verse gives us the answer to where dirt is good and what it does that is good."

"What does it say, Grandma?" Bobbie asked that, but I wanted to know about good dirt too.

"'And God said, Let the earth bring forth grass, the herb that yields seed, and the fruit tree that yields fruit according to its kind, whose seed is in itself, on the earth; and it was so. . . . And God saw that it was good.' When dirt is outside, it's wonderful. It helps bring us fruit, vegetables, trees, grass and flowers. But Megan's right; dirt doesn't do much good inside."

Megan got the broom. "All right, then, I'm going to put this dirt back where it belongs!"

QUESTIONS TO ASK YOUR CHILD

1. Who made the dirt?
2. What does God call the dirt?
3. Why do we need to have dirt?

How Did
We Get Day?

"But I don't want to go to bed. Why can't we have daytime all the time?" Bobbie never wants to go to bed. She likes to play outside all the time. She always asks Megan and me to take long walks with her.

"Bobbie, you played hard all day, and right now you're grouchy because you're tired and need some rest."

"No I don't. I'm not tired, and I don't want to go to bed—not now or ever."

Mom told her, "Well, tomorrow is a big day, and you need your rest to enjoy all the fun things I have planned for you."

Bobbie wanted to stall so she wouldn't have to go to bed. "How did we get day, Mom?" she asked.

"God made it for us."

"Why?"

"Well, in the beginning of time it was dark everywhere all the time."

"Yuck! I wouldn't want to live then, would you?"

"Actually, nobody could live then because the earth was empty. There was no light or earth or sky or sun or moon or stars or anything except God."

"Did God invent light, Mom?"

"Not exactly; He made it."

"What did He make light out of?" Bobbie wanted to know.

"God used nothing."

"Nothing? How did He do that?"

"The Bible says that God spoke and the light was there."

"Wow, that's like magic!"

"No, Bobbie, that's like God. He enjoys making something out of nothing. It's not magic; it's God's great power."

"Does God like light?"

"The Bible tells us He thinks it is good."

"Me too!"

QUESTIONS TO ASK YOUR CHILD

1. What was it like before God made day?
2. How did God make light?
3. Can you make something out of nothing? Why not?

Why Is Night Dark?

"Children, it's time to come in!"

"It's still light out, and you said we could play till dark," said Toph.

"I know I said that, but it's getting close to 8:30, and you haven't even had your baths yet. It'll be after nine by the time you get ready for bed."

Toph wanted to obey, but he argued. "It's summer, and we don't have school tomorrow."

"Yes, but we have a busy day planned for tomorrow, and I don't want you to be grumpy halfway through the day. So please stop arguing and come in right now."

"OK, we're coming." Megan, Bobbie and Toph went up the stairs and into the house. Bobbie took her bath first. She was in there forever before Mom peeked around the bathroom door.

"Bobbie, look at your fingers and toes! Look how wrinkled they are. Isn't it time for you to get out of the tub?"

"It's not time yet."

"Bobbie, you have been in there for half an hour, and it is time. Get out right now, and I'll help dry you. It's getting late, and besides it's completely dark now so you can sleep."

Mom patted Bobbie dry with a towel. "Did you get a new bulb for the night-light, Mom?"

Mom stopped to think. "Oh, I'm sorry, Bobbie, I forgot."

They went into Bobbie's room. "But Mom, it's so dark that I can't fall asleep." Bobbie really hates the dark.

Mom told her, "Well, you'll have to try to go to sleep because all the stores are closed now and it's way past your bedtime."

"Mom, why is night dark?" Bobbie asked while Mom tucked her into bed.

"Because God made it that way."

"Why?"

"So we would know it wasn't day."

"Why can't it be day all the time?"

"It says somewhere in the Bible that God made the darkness, and then it's nighttime. During the night the animals of the forest come out."

"Yikes! Are there wild animals in our backyard at night? I'm scared." She gets scared pretty easily.

"No, Bobbie." Mom hugged her. "The wildest animals we have are squirrels. But God did make some animals that are nocturnal."

"What's 'nocturnal'?"

"'Nocturnal' means they see better and move around better at night. There are day creatures and night creatures."

"Mom, are people day creatures or night creatures?"

"They're day creatures, and you need to get to sleep." Mom kissed Bobbie good-night. "I'll tell you what," she said, "you be still now, and I'll sing you a bedtime song."

QUESTIONS TO ASK YOUR CHILD

1. Who made the darkness?
2. What is the darkness called?
3. Why did God make the darkness?

Do Fish Breathe?

Sea World is one of my favorite places. We have a season pass, and we go anytime someone comes to visit us during the summer. My favorite part is the great white whale. When he splashes, everyone in the stands gets a bath. I think it's funny!

Megan says she likes the sea lions. They can balance a ball on their noses, clap their flippers and jump way high out of the water. They play tag in the water, and they play volleyball with a big ball. Dad told me they are really smart animals.

Bobbie likes the dolphins. She says they talk. They do make sounds, but I don't think they are talking like people talk. One time when we went to Sea World, Bobbie got picked to go down and get a kiss from one of the dolphins. She laughed so hard she almost fell over. The trainer even let Bobbie feed the dolphins. When Bobbie came back to her seat, she asked Mom, "How do fish breathe? I don't see a nose on them." I couldn't see any noses either.

"God made them so they can live in the water. Some fish are mammals, like whales and dolphins. They feed their babies with milk from the mother. They also come to the top of the water to get air. Other fish breathe water through their gills, those slits on the sides of their heads."

"Did God make every fish in Sea World? That's a lot!"

"Well, God did not speak to make each fish that you see here, but He did make each of the kinds of fish and mammals that swim. He made all the sea creatures at creation."

"What's creation?"

"That's when God made everything in the world in one week."

"How many days make a week?"

I answered that question. "Seven."

"Did God make all the fish in seven days, Mom?"

"Well, actually He did it during just one of the days of that week. He is so powerful that all He had to do was speak a word, and all the different kinds were created."

"God just said 'fish,' and they were there?"

"Something like that."

"God is smart and strong. I'm glad He made fish so they can breathe in water. I got some water in my nose in the bathtub last night. It hurt my nose! I can't be a fish."

QUESTIONS TO ASK YOUR CHILD

1. What is creation?
2. How did God make all the sea creatures?
3. How do fish breathe?

What's Your Favorite Animal?

My class took a trip to the Cleveland Zoo. Mrs. Peters, our teacher, gave us permission slips to have our parents sign. She even asked for some mothers to come along to help. My mom wanted to go, and I was glad. Tommy's mom went too. We were supposed to pick a favorite animal. And for homework, we had to write a story about how that animal came to be like it is.

Tommy changed his mind with each new animal he saw. First he was going to write about the orangutans, until we got to the ape house. That big black creature was so strong and yet so gentle with its little baby. The lions and tigers were loud and scary. They roared and roared so loud we had to cover our ears. The zebras were like painted horses and made me dizzy when they ran around.

The elephants were huge and used their trunks like hands to pick up peanuts and hay and even sucked water like a vacuum. The yaks were interesting with their large horns and strong bodies that looked like an ox. We also saw camels, deer and turtles.

The reptile house was the greatest. I liked all the giant lizards. The girls were scared and wouldn't open their eyes for very long. Tommy and I came up behind some girls and touched their backs—hardly at all—when they walked by the snakes. They screamed super loud! Girls don't like creeping things, you know.

We saw a lot of birds. I got all confused trying to remember their names. Everywhere we went, we could push a button and hear a tape recording tell about that animal.

When I got home, I decided to write about the platypus. I remembered some things the tape at the zoo said. I just wasn't sure what it meant.

I asked Mom if the platypus was millions of years old.

"Why do you ask?"

"I'm writing my paper for Mrs. Peters. The tape recording in the zoo said 'this animal helps to prove evolution.' It said the platypus is millions of years old and is learning to go from land animal to sea animal. What is evolution anyway?"

"It's an idea that some men who don't love or believe in God thought up. They try to explain away the mighty work that God did in creation."

"So you don't think animals evolutioned?"

"The word is 'evolved,' Topher. And, no, I don't. Neither does the Bible. I believe the Word of God tells us the truth about how all the animals were created."

I still wondered about the platypus. "How did we get such a strange animal then?"

"God loves colors and variety. I also think He enjoys His creation."

I thought God was always serious. I didn't think He smiled. So I asked Mom if God had fun sometimes.

"Genesis tells us that God made every living creature on the earth, including platypuses. He made every single kind of animal—even the funny-looking ones."

"But how do we get so many like we have today?"

"The number of kinds of animals hasn't changed over the years, Toph, but each kind has babies of its own kind."

"But I think the kids at school believe evolution. If I don't write it in my paper, Mrs. Peters might laugh or give me a bad grade or something."

"Actually, son, you might be surprised. Many people say they believe in evolution until someone challenges them with the truth. Even Charles Darwin, who first wrote about evolution, changed his mind before he died."

"Really, Mom?"

"Really. Maybe you could include that little fact in your paper. Let me find a book that tells about him. Besides, who always tells the truth, God or man?"

"God, of course!"

Verse to Read

1 Corinthians 15:39: "All flesh is not the same flesh, but there is one kind of flesh of men, another flesh of beasts [animals], another of fish, and another of birds" (NKJV).

QUESTIONS TO ASK YOUR CHILD

1. What is evolution?
2. How were animals created?
3. Who is telling the truth about how animals were made—God or people who believe in evolution?

Were People Ever Animals?

"Mom, how do you spell Melissa?" Megan was making invitations to Bobbie's birthday party.

"M-e-l-i-s-s-a."

"I thought so. How do you spell Carrie?"

"C-a-r-r-i-e. Do you need some help?"

"I just want to check that I'm spelling the names right. You told me to finish the invitations by today." Megan has to have everything perfect. She was checking every single letter when the phone rang. Mom answered it.

"Yes, the party is Saturday at two, in our backyard. . . . Oh, we plan to play a few animal games and have cake and ice cream. Melissa is welcome to stay a little later until you get back from the mall." Mom must have been talking to Mrs. Jones.

A week later Bobbie skipped around the living room and sang, "Today's my day! Today's my day!" It was Saturday, and her friends were coming for a birthday party. She was so excited she was acting pretty goofy. "Toph, want to see me roll over? I can roll over like a monkey." She rolled over and laughed.

At the party, Mom explained how to play the first game. "Let's play animal-upset-the-zoo-basket. I'll give each of you an animal name. When I call your animal, leave your seat and try to find another seat. The last one standing is out for one turn. Ready?" Bobbie and her friends looked like they had fun playing that game.

"Next let's play the barnyard animal game. I will whisper the name of an animal in your ear. When I clap my hands, you make the sound of that animal and find everyone else who is your same animal. CLAP, CLAP." The backyard sounded like a real zoo.

After that game, Bobbie blew out the candles on her cake. Megan and Toph gave everyone a plate with cake and ice cream on it and a cup of punch. Then Bobbie opened her presents.

That night Bobbie was still excited. "That was the funnest party! Can we do it next year?"

Mom didn't look too excited. "I'm still very tired from all the work. We'll wait and see."

"Oh Mom, I want to do it again. Did you see Carrie being a monkey?"

"Yes, she did a convincing job. She sure made you laugh with her jungle sounds."

"Mom, can people really be animals?"

Mom said, "No. They can pretend like you did today."

"But were people ever animals for real?"

"Some people say that man was once a monkey and that slowly over thousands of years his hair fell out and he began walking more and walking straighter."

"Mom, is it true? Was I once a monkey?"

"No, Bobbie, it isn't true at all. If people were once monkeys, we shouldn't still have monkeys around. They all should have changed into people at the same time. Besides, the Bible tells us that God made people and animals differently."

"How did He make animals, Mom?"

"In the Bible, the book of Genesis tells us that God spoke and animals were made from nothing."

"How did God make people?"

"Genesis says that God used the dust of the ground to make man. God did something for man that He didn't do for any of His other creatures."

"What?"

"God breathed into man and gave Adam the breath of life. Man and animals are different and will never be the same. People are in God's likeness—they live forever. Animals live and die, and that's the end of them."

"What did God make first?"

"God waited till last to make man, because he was the most important creature God made. God made everything else for Adam and Eve to enjoy. I know some people act like animals sometimes, but they can never be animals for real."

"I don't really want to be an animal. I'm glad I'm a people. God made me special."

QUESTIONS TO ASK YOUR CHILD

1. What is the difference between the way God made animals and people?
2. Was man ever an animal?
3. Which is more important to God— people or animals?

3

I Have a Question About the
BIBLE

Hints and Helps

Christianity is essentially a faith in which God reveals Himself. Exodus 3:4 provides an example in which God spoke plainly and openly to His servant Moses. Numerous other times God spoke audibly from Heaven to His creatures. God sometimes dispatched angel messengers or sent earthly messengers. These occasions complement the ultimate communication of God to man in Jesus Christ. Jesus, the Son of God, came to earth. His words from God fill most of the books of Matthew, Mark, Luke and John. Furthermore, the whole Bible is the complete message from God to us.

Verse to Memorize
  2 Timothy 3:16: "All Scripture is God-breathed and is useful for teaching, rebuking, correcting and training in righteousness" (NIV).

Does the Bible Have Pictures?

Mom takes us to the library once a week. I don't like to go, until I get there. Then it's OK. Megan loves to go. She always beats Bobbie and me to the car. She takes this huge book bag to hold all the books she finds.

Bobbie can't read at all because she's only four. But she says she loves books too. That's because Megan or Mom reads and reads and reads to her. Sometimes at night after I can't play outside anymore, I read to Bobbie too.

Bobbie tries to read the pictures. Sometimes when I go by her room, I hear her "reading" to her dolls and stuffed animals. She puts them in a row on her bed and "reads" to them from the pictures. When we go to the library, Bobbie just picks the books with the best pictures.

A little while after her birthday, Bobbie got a package in the mail. It had "Bobbie Schmidt, 1022 Brewster Court, Grafton, Ohio," written on it. It was from Grandpa Williams in Pennsylvania! Bobbie went crazy when she saw it. I wanted to know what it was too. Grandpa and Grandma had already given Bobbie a birthday present.

Bobbie ripped off the paper and found a book. She didn't know what it was, so she showed it to Mom. Mom told her it was a children's Bible. Then Mom opened to the first page and read a note from Grandpa. It said, "Joshua 1:8. This book will be the best one you could ever read."

Bobbie looked kind of confused. "Why does Grandpa say that, Mom?"

"Let's read the verse and find out." Mom read the verse from the Bible. Then she told us, "It says we must never quit talking or thinking about this book. If we keep thinking about it, we'll have a prosperous way and good success."

"What's 'prosprous way' mean?" I didn't know that word either.

"Pros-per-ous." Mom said the word the right way because Bobbie had said it wrong. "Prosperous usually means rich, but here it means doing really well. It means if we keep talking about and thinking about the Bible, we'll have a good life."

I wanted to have a good life. So I told Mom, "Then we should read the Bible a lot."

Mom looked a little sad. "I used to read the Bible all the time when I was a girl. Bobbie, maybe you and I can read from your new Bible every night before you go to bed."

Bobbie didn't seem too excited. "Does this Bible book have pictures?"

Mom took the Bible. "Yes, it does in several ways." She turned some pages and gave it back to Bobbie. "Here, look for yourself."

I looked too. There was a picture of a man with lions standing around him. Bobbie turned some more pages. "Here's a picture of a man and a big funny-looking boat." Bobbie let me turn some more pages, and I found a picture of a boy throwing a rock at a huge giant. A few pages later we found another picture. "Here's a lady and man with a baby in a barn," Bobbie told Mom. "And here's a man with children all around Him. He looks nice." Bobbie turned some more pages, and we saw a sad picture. She gave the book to Mom. "What's this a picture of?"

"That man with the tied hands is on trial," Mom told us. She gave the Bible back to us. Bobbie let me turn the pages again. "Look, Bobbie! A picture of angels and a giant rock!" Bobbie liked that picture. But then we couldn't find any more.

"That's all the pictures." Bobbie closed the book.

But Mom said, "There's more, Bobbie."

I knew there weren't. So I told Mom, "No there's not."

"Yes there is. Let me show you. The Bible is full of pictures told in stories. Jesus loved to tell picture stories called parables. Here's one in Luke about a sheep and a coin."

"Like Grandpa's sheep and Topher's coins?"

"Yes, like that, Bobbie."

Verses to Read

Luke 15:3–10

Take time to explain that the lost sheep pictures lost people away from God. The lost coin is like lost people whom God seeks and finds.

Young children take things quite literally and will not comprehend the truth behind the parables. However, they can enjoy the picture stories, and later as they mature, they will understand the meaning.

QUESTIONS TO ASK YOUR CHILD

1. What is the best book you could ever read?
2. What is a picture story called?
3. How often should you read the Bible?

What Does
'Holy Bible' Mean?

Megan has been saying, "You can tell a book by its cover." I think she heard the lady at the library say that, so now she says it too. Anyway, I didn't know what that meant until we were at the library one day. Megan showed us *Curious George* and *Clifford the Big Red Dog* and *101 Dalmatians*, *Cyrus the Incredible Sea Serpent* and *Are You My Mother?* The pictures and words on the front of the books told us what was inside. You could tell that Curious George is a nosy monkey—that's what 'curious' means. He gets into trouble all the time. Clifford is a huge dog.

Dalmatians are dogs too, and there are 101 of them in that book. At least there were supposed to be 101; I didn't really count them. Cyrus is the silliest sea serpent you'll ever see. And the bird who asked the question "Are you my mother?" kind of reminded me of Bobbie!

My favorite books are the Hardy Boys mystery books. My dad reads them to me. I guess you can tell from the cover that it's a mystery book. The picture tells that, because it's kind of scary but not really. The Hardy Boys get into a mystery every time. Sometime I'm going to have adventures like theirs.

When Megan got done showing us the books, Bobbie was really quiet. I wondered if she was sick or something. She's hardly ever quiet. I guess she was thinking about her new Bible from Grandpa. She finally asked, "Megan, what does my Bible say on the cover?"

"I don't know, but we can look when we get home."

"But can you tell what the Bible is about from its cover?" Bobbie wanted to know.

I was trying to remember. "I think it has a picture of a man dressed in a robe. He's sitting on a rock, and there's lots of children and some words. But I'm not sure."

Mom came then and helped us check out our books. When we got home, Bobbie went upstairs. Megan and I went too. Bobbie keeps her Bible next to her bed because Mom reads the stories at night before she goes to sleep. Bobbie looked at her Bible and showed it to Megan.

"Toph, you're right." Megan doesn't tell me that very much. "Here's a man." She pointed to the cover. "He's with some children. He looks gentle and kind. His clothes seem kind of funny, but the children have clothes like us. Let's ask Mom who he is."

Bobbie grabbed her Bible from Megan and ran downstairs to the kitchen. We followed her. "Mom, who is the man on the front of my new Bible?"

"Oh, that's Jesus."

"How come He's dressed in that beach robe?"

Mom smiled. "That's a tunic, not a beach robe. Jesus lived a long time ago and a long way from here. It's very hot in Israel where Jesus was born. Men wore long, loose clothes to protect them from the sun. Some men over there still wear robes. They're usually white to keep the men cool."

"But the children have clothes like us."

"Jesus loves children from long ago and from now too. The cover shows Jesus with children of today to show kids who read the Bible that He loves them too."

"Oh. What do the words on my Bible cover say?"

"They say 'HOLY BIBLE.'"

"What's that mean, Mom?"

"Well, 'holy' is a word that means 'set apart for a special purpose.' The Bible is a very special book. It's the best book in the world. It tells us about God and what He's like."

I couldn't figure something out. So I asked, "Is the Bible about God or Jesus?"

"Actually, it's about both of them and how they love people. It tells how we can get to Heaven to live with God and Jesus forever."

Bobbie sounded excited. "I want to see Jesus and sit on His lap like that girl on the cover. What does 'Bible' mean, Mom?"

"'Bible' means 'the book.' It is the writing about God. God saw to it that the men who wrote the Bible put down exactly what He wanted in His book. They did not make any mistakes because God was really the author."

"The Bible tells about God and Jesus and people and Heaven?"

"Yes, it's about all that and much more."

QUESTIONS TO ASK YOUR CHILD

1. What does "holy" mean?
2. What does the Bible tell you about God and Jesus?
3. Name one thing you have learned from the Bible.

Is the Bible
for Kids?

On Saturday mornings Mom takes us to the grocery store to buy our food for the week. One Saturday Megan and Bobbie started bugging Mom to buy stuff.

We started by the milk. "Can we get chocolate milk, Mom?" Megan asked that. She loves everything chocolate. I guess I do too.

But Mom said, "No, let's make our own from the chocolate syrup we already have."

When we turned the corner, Bobbie saw a big picture of cookies. "Can we get those cookies with white stuff in the middle?"

"No, Bobbie, I plan to bake your favorite cookies this afternoon while you take your nap." Mom went really fast down the cookie aisle. I think it was so we wouldn't ask for anything else.

"Yea for cookies, yuck for nap. Cookies are for kids, Mom. Naps are for babies." Bobbie was getting a little crabby already.

"I like to take a nap sometimes." Mom wheeled the cart down the cereal aisle.

"Yeah, but you're old. Naps are not for kids my age."

Megan grabbed some cereal. "Mom, can we get Trix and Captain Crunch?"

"Let's pick cereal that everyone likes so we can all eat it."

"But Dad likes Trix, and Toph loves Captain Crunch." She was right. So Mom said, "OK."

When we got to the freezer part, Bobbie started bugging Mom again. "Ice cream! Can we get some, Mom?"

"What kind of ice cream do children like?" Mom smiled at us.

"Any kind!" Bobbie said.

"What kind do you think grown-ups like?"

Megan could answer that. She seemed to know what everyone liked. "Dad says any kind of ice cream will do."

Mom nodded her head. But then she asked, "So when do you get too old to eat ice cream?"

"Never. I want to eat it till I'm a hundred zillion years old!" Bobbie said.

Even Mom laughed at that. Then I asked Mom, "How come grown-ups and kids like some things the same and some things different?"

"I think it has something to do with their stomachs and the taste buds in their mouths."

Bobbie opened her mouth really wide. "What are taste buds, Mom? Do I have some?"

"Yes you do, Bobbie. They help us taste our food. As we grow, they change. The kinds of food we like change too. It seems like our taste for sweets never changes though."

Mom finished the shopping and paid the lady at the register. When we got

out to the car, Bobbie had another question.

"Mom, is the Bible for kids or for grown-ups?"

"You know what? Let's call Grandpa when we get home and ask him. He likes to answer your questions about the Bible."

Bobbie wanted Mom to call Grandpa right away, but Mom made her wait until all the food was put away. Then Bobbie ran to the phone. She held it to her ear while Mom dialed the number.

"Hello, Grandpa. This is Bobbie." She didn't even give Grandpa a chance to say hello. "Is the Bible for kids or for grown-ups?"

"It's for everybody. But some parts of it are harder than others. The Bible talks about teaching God's Word to little children, young people and adults. Moms and dads and grandmas and grandpas are supposed to tell their children and grandchildren all about God's ways."

"Why?"

"So they'll know more about God. So they'll know how to love Him and obey Him. So they'll come to trust Him as their Savior."

"What's 'Savior,' Grandpa?"

"Jesus is the Savior. He came to earth to die on the cross for us. God would have had to punish us for our sins. Sins are the wrong things we do. But Jesus took the punishment for us."

"Is the Savior for kids too?"

"Yes, He sure is."

Verses to Read

  2 Timothy 3:15: "And that from a child thou hast known the holy scriptures, which are able to make thee wise unto salvation through faith which is in Christ Jesus."

  Psalm 119:9: "Wherewithal shall a young man cleanse his way? by taking heed thereto according to thy word."

  Luke 2:36, 37: "And there was one Anna . . . : she was of great age . . . [who] departed not from the temple, but served God with fastings and prayers night and day."

  Deuteronomy 6:6, 7: "And these words, which I command thee this day, shall be in thine heart: And thou shalt teach them diligently unto thy children, and shalt talk of them when thou sittest in thine house, and when thou walkest by the way, and when thou liest down, and when thou risest up."

QUESTIONS TO ASK YOUR CHILD

1. Whom is the Bible for?
2. Who is the Savior, and what did He do for you?
3. Do you need a Savior?

Do You Read the Bible?

One Saturday Mom was in a bad mood because the house was a mess and company was coming. There were papers and magazines and books everywhere—on the end tables, on the couch and chairs in the living room, by the beds. Dad even had a bunch of newspapers in the garage. Mom asked everyone to help.

Toph wanted to play with Tommy, but he knew he should help Mom. So he talked to Tommy, and Tommy said he would help too. The boys decided to get all the papers together and ask Tommy's brother Jim to drive them to the recycling place. They thought they might even get some money!

Megan asked Mom if she could look through all the magazines and tear out the pictures. She said she wanted to take them to school to use in art class. Mom thought that was a good idea.

"I'll take the books we've already read to the library," Dad told Mom. "Bobbie, you can help me find them." When Bobbie went into her room, she saw her Bible by her bed. She remembered that Dad had said he would return all the books the family had already read. Bobbie and Mom read that Bible every night, so Bobbie put her Bible in the book bag.

Bobbie found Megan's and Toph's library books, too, and put them in the book bag. Finally she got Mom's two big books from beside her bed.

Dad and Bobbie went to the library before lunch. Dad drove up to the door and let Bobbie go up to the book drop. She always drops just one book at a time because it makes a clunk noise when it hits the bottom. Bobbie put in all the books from the bag. CLUNK! CLUNK! CLUNK! CLUNK!

That night after the company had left, Mom helped Bobbie get ready for bed. "Thanks so much for helping me clean up today. You sure did a good job here in your room. Let's read from the Bible before you go to bed." Mom looked around. "Bobbie, where's your Bible?"

"I turned it in to the library today."

"You what?"

"I turned it in to the library today with the other books."

"Bobbie, that was your special book from Grandpa."

"I know, but you said we had books all over the house and they were making a mess."

"I didn't mean your Bible."

"But we've already read it. Remember? Dad said we should take back the books we've already read."

"Bobbie, the Bible is the kind of book that you read over and over again."

"Really?"

"Yes! It has so many wonderful things about God, and every time you read it, it can help you."

"How can we get my Bible back?"

"I'll call the library first thing in the morning."

Mom kissed Bobbie good-night. Bobbie pulled the covers up high like she always does and smiled.

Verses to Read

Psalm 119:10, 11: "With my whole heart have I sought thee: O let me not wander from thy commandments. Thy word have I hid in [my] heart, that I might not sin against thee."

Psalm 119:97: "O how I love thy law! it is my meditation all the day."

QUESTIONS TO ASK YOUR CHILD

1. What book should you read over and over again?
2. Why should you read the Bible?

How Old
Is the Bible?

Last summer when we visited Grandma and Grandpa, I had this thing about finding out how old things are. I asked Grandma about all of the dishes in her kitchen. Then I asked about the old vases she keeps on this special shelf in the dining room. I guess she's been collecting them since she was a little girl. The really old ones have a date on the bottom. I found one that said 1898!

Grandpa let me look at his books too. He showed me how to look in the front to find out when the book was written. I found a super old one from

1908. The pages were yellow! Grandpa told me to be very careful when I turned the pages so I wouldn't tear them. When I was done looking at the books, Grandpa told me to follow him.

He took me to the sheep barn. "Know how old these sheep are, son?"

"That one looks smaller than this one, but I don't know how old they are. How can you tell?"

"You count teeth!"

I thought Grandpa must be kidding. "Count teeth?"

But I guessed it was true when Grandpa got down on his knees and opened the mouth of a small ewe—you know, a girl sheep. I sat down next to him. "Here take a look. This one has two big teeth; that means she is one year old. Sheep have two big teeth for every one year." I had studied multiplication in the third grade, so I knew what that meant.

I got another ewe. I will tell you that I was kind of scared, but I opened its mouth. "This one has four big teeth, Grandpa." *Four teeth divided by two means* . . . "Does that mean she's two years old?"

Grandpa nodded his head. "You've got the idea. And this one has six big teeth. Can you guess how old she might be, Topher?"

Six teeth divided by two equals . . . "Three!"

"You're right, son."

Grandpa and I talked about a bunch of other stuff while I helped him with the chores. When we got back to the house, I picked up Grandpa's Bible and sat in his big chair. Grandpa's Bible is so huge I have to hold it with both hands. "How old is this Bible, Grandpa?"

"Oh, a couple thousand years old." He sat down on the couch since I was in his favorite chair.

"A couple thousand? Are you kidding me?"

"No, actually it is."

"Then who wrote it?"

"The Bible is actually 66 books. Many people over many years helped to write it. God used Moses and Paul and many other men. The Bible covers the time of the Pharaohs in Egypt when Moses wrote, to the time of Jesus' friend John, who wrote the book called Revelation."

I couldn't believe it was so old. "How was it kept for so long?"

"Well, special people called scribes worked to make copies of the books in the Bible."

"They just copied the words from one place to another?"

"Right, son."

"I hate doing that! When I get in trouble at school, I have to write the same sentence a hundred times. It's boring and hard, Grandpa."

"It is indeed, but those scribes loved God so much that they copied the Bible to worship God and to make sure other people got to read the Bible. One way they wrote was with quill pens—that's the tip of a feather dipped in ink. They wrote on papyrus, a kind of paper made from tall grasses."

"Why didn't they use a printing press or something like that?" I know about printing presses from a field trip we took to a newspaper place.

"Printing presses weren't invented yet. Not until very, very, very much later."

"Did a scribe copy this Bible?"

Grandpa smiled when I asked that. "No, the scribes' copies must be very brittle. They would fall apart too easily—like the yellow pages in that old book you looked at this morning. The scribes' copies are kept in special museums for people to study."

"Then this Bible isn't really a couple thousand years old, Grandpa."

"No, not this copy, but the Bible itself is a couple thousand years old. Down through the centuries scholars have accurately copied and translated the words into languages like our English."

"What does 'accurately' mean?"

"'Accurately' means without any mistakes. The words are almost identical to the first copies."

"But what does 'identical' mean?" Grandpa uses big words sometimes.

"'Identical' means 'exactly the same.'"

"Someday I'm going to go to that museum and see the words that Moses wrote." It sounded like a good adventure.

"Well, son, I'm afraid that one is long gone. But we have enough copies to know for sure that we have the true message. God made sure of that."

Verse to Read

Psalm 119:89: "For ever, O LORD, thy word is settled in heaven."

QUESTIONS TO ASK YOUR CHILD

1. How old is the Bible?
2. Who were the scribes?
3. How can you be sure you have the true Bible?

Who Wrote
the Bible?

I think history is the hardest subject, especially when the teacher shows a picture of a building and asks us to guess what it is and who it stands for. I know the Lincoln Memorial stands for Abraham Lincoln. He was a famous president. I know the Washington Monument stands for George Washington, the first president of the United States. I know the Jefferson Memorial too. Thomas Jefferson wrote the Declaration of Independence.

Megan's super smart. She knows all those buildings and the people they

stand for. She knows about the people who write children's books too. She knows who wrote the Nancy Drew series and the Hardy Boys books. She knows Beverly Cleary and Dr. Seuss. She knows about the Berenstains too. They're the ones who wrote the Berenstain Bears books. And she even knows all about Richard Scarry, who wrote *Cars and Trucks and Things That Go.*

One day Megan got the idea to set her books on the bookshelf according to the person who wrote them. First she dumped all the books on the floor. Then Megan put them together by who wrote them. Bobbie wanted to help Megan, so she handed the books to Megan, and Megan put them on the shelf. She put all her Berenstain Bear books on the first shelf. Then she put the Walt Disney books on the second shelf, and the beginner readers went next to them. She put her Dr. Seuss books together too. You can always tell a Dr. Seuss book because it has a goofy picture and a funny title like *Yurtle the Turtle.*

When Megan set the last book on the shelf, Bobbie jumped up and ran to her room. She came back with the children's Bible Grandpa had sent her. "Where would my Bible go, Megan?"

"Well, I think God wrote it, but let's go ask Mom." They went downstairs. Mom was putting the dishes away.

"Mom, who wrote my Bible?"

Megan told Mom why she was asking that. "Bobbie and I are putting the books by author, and we need to know."

"Moses, Isaiah, Jeremiah, David, Solomon, Matthew, Mark, Luke, John, Peter, Paul, to begin with." Mom smiled—I think because Megan looked so surprised.

"How could so many people write one book?"

"Well, the Bible is more like a library with many books. It has 66 all together. Over 40 different men wrote at least one book in it."

"Then all of their names should be on the book cover."

"Well, they aren't, because in another way God is the author."

Bobbie didn't get it. "Was it God or those other guys?"

"It's both at the same time. The books have the style of the different writers. It's like you can tell the difference between a Dr. Seuss book and a Berenstain Bears book without knowing the author. The people who wrote the books have different styles. God guided the Bible writers to write exactly what God wanted us to know."

"Is it like dictation in spelling class?" Megan was trying to figure it out.

"No, it's not like that. The writers of the Bible were holy men, and God's

Spirit helped them as they wrote—like a wind blows, or carries, a boat along. The wind doesn't make the boat; it only moves it along in a path."

"So those Bible guys wrote what God wanted, but like they would say it." That kind of made sense. Megan was quiet for a second, but then she told Bobbie to come with her. "Let's put the Bible on the shelf under 'G' for God."

Verses to Read

2 Peter 1:21: "For the prophecy came not in old time by the will of man: but holy men of God spake as they were moved by the Holy Ghost."

2 Timothy 3:16: "All Scripture is given by inspiration of God, and is profitable. . . ."

QUESTIONS TO ASK YOUR CHILD
1. How many men wrote the Bible?
2. Who helped the men to write?

Does the Bible
Have Mistakes?

One day after school I went into the kitchen. Mom was fixing supper, and Bobbie was on the floor coloring. I had to ask a favor. "Mom, I need to take my science book back to school tomorrow. Will you help me remember?"

"Sure, Toph. Is there a problem?"

"Mrs. Peters says our book has mistakes in it." I showed my old book to Mom. "We're going to get a new one that's 'more up-to-date and accurate.' " I tried to make my voice sound like Mrs. Peters when I said that. I guess

I sounded a little bit like her, but not really.

Mom looked at the book. "It is an older book. The cover is worn out from all the children who have used it. What's the year inside the cover, Toph?"

"It says 1987, Mom. That isn't very old."

"For a science book it is. We find out new things so fast that every seven years we know twice as much information."

I guess Bobbie had been listening for a while. But then she stopped coloring and left the kitchen without saying anything. She must have gone to her room to find the Bible Grandpa had sent her.

She picked it up and looked at it. That must have been when she started to cry. She was taking her Bible to the garage-sale box when she passed Dad. He was working in his shop in the garage. Dad saw Bobbie's tears. "Bobbie, what are you doing?"

She sniffed and wiped a tear from her cheek. "I'm gettin' riduff an ol' book thas oud-duff-date. It's prob'ly full of 'stakes like Toph's science book." Bobbie sounds funny when she's been crying.

"And why are you crying, little one?"

" 'Cause I luff to read it wiff Mom every night." Dad gave her a Kleenex™, and Bobbie blew her nose.

"Let me see that book, please." Bobbie showed Dad the book. "Why, Bobbie, that's your new Bible! What are you doing with it?"

"I'm—I'm . . . " Then Bobbie hiccuped. "I'm taking it to the garage-sale box so Mom can sell it."

"But why would you do that?"

" 'Cause Mom told Topher that old books have 'stakes. And Grandpa said the Bible is really old. It must be filled with 'stakes."

"The Bible is old. And many people think the Bible does have mistakes and is untrue in places, but they are wrong. God wrote the Bible, and God never has to find anything out. People wrote the science book, and people are always learning new things. God made everything and knows everything. There's nothing new to Him. His book is true and right forever. The Bible even says that the earth will fall apart and that the Bible will still be true."

"Is the earth going to fall apart?"

"Not today, Bobbie. And you don't need to sell your Bible. It will be true forever." Dad gave Bobbie one of his big hugs—the kind where you can hardly breathe.

"Thanks, Dad. I didn't want to sell it." When Bobbie came back to the kitchen, she was singing really loud. I think she made up the song. "This is my Bible. I can keep it forever. It's always true."

Verses to Memorize

Psalm 119:160: "Thy word is true from the beginning: and every one of thy righteous judgments endureth forever."

Matthew 5:18: "I tell you the truth, until heaven and earth disappear, not the smallest letter, not the least stroke of a pen, will by any means disappear from the Law until everything is accomplished" (NIV).

QUESTIONS TO ASK YOUR CHILD

1. How is the Bible different from any other book?
2. How long will God's Word be true?

4

I Have a Question About
JESUS CHRIST

Hints and Helps

With this subject we reach an intricate and difficult problem. Orthodox Christianity has always believed in the doctrine of the Trinity. And we do too! But believing and explaining are sometimes extremely different tasks, especially when it comes to children. We will talk with you the adult about the Trinity. We will not endeavor to do the same with the children. But children can be good theologians, and they will ask you about the Trinity.

The Trinity is a tri-unity of persons. Historic Christianity teaches that God is one as manifested in three distinct Persons: "The LORD our God, the LORD is one!" (Deuteronomy 6:4; NKJV). Yet the Great Commission in Matthew 28:19 and 20 includes the baptismal formula that teaches that God is the Father, the Son and the Holy Spirit. Three persons yet one God! The structure of the language in Matthew strongly points out that each of these three Persons is equal.

What's in a name? Everything! Parents often subtly predict the personality of their children when they choose their names. The name of God's Son is the Lord Jesus Christ. He has other titles as well; each title is significant. "Lord" means Master. "Jesus" is a Greek form of the Hebrew name Joshua, which means Jehovah is salvation. "Jehovah" is God's covenantal, or relational, name to His special people Israel. "Christ" denotes Jesus' deity. It literally means "the anointed one."

By application of Jesus' names, we know that the Lord Jesus Christ desires to be three things in our lives. As Lord, Jesus desires to be the Master of your life. As Jesus, He longs to be your Savior from sin and punishment. As Christ, He is very God taking on the form of man. Therefore, He is familiar with all your limitations, sorrows and sin without being touched or tainted by sin (Heb. 4:14–16).

Christianity is based on faith. Part of faith is believing in the Trinity simply because, according to Scriptures, God is triune. We believe in a triune God simply because He declares Himself to be so, not because we fully comprehend the Trinity. If we could explain God, He wouldn't be God.

What Is Jesus Like?

Mom plays "Who Am I?" with us all the time. She describes a person, an animal or a thing and asks, "What am I?" Then we have to guess what it is.

One day when we were going to the library, Mom said, "Who am I? I have four legs. I like to eat grass. I give milk. I make a loud sound with my mouth."

"A cow!"

"Good, Bobbie, you guessed it. Now who am I? I have two legs. I do my work by walking and sometimes riding in a car. I carry a large pack on my

shoulder. I visit many houses each day."

I thought I knew that one. "Is it a paperboy?"

"Nice try, son, but that's not what I have in mind. When driving the car, this person sometimes drives on the wrong side of the street."

I was about to say a mailman, but Megan said it first.

"Yes, that's it. Good guess, Megan."

"Who am I?" Mom asked us again. "I live in your yard. I am green."

"Grass?"

"No, but keep guessing, Bobbie. I have a trunk and long arms. I turn colors in the fall."

"A tree!" Bobbie shouted it. She shouts the answer a lot. She gets so excited.

"Right, Bobbie. And now who am I? I have four legs. People use me when they eat. I am in your dining room."

"Is it a chair?" Megan asked.

Mom looked in the rearview mirror so she could see us in the backseat. "No, but you're very close. People put food and plates on me while they eat."

Then I knew the answer. "A table!"

"Right, Toph." Then Mom thought for a second. "Who am I? I have two legs. I like to walk. The Bible talks about me, mostly in the New Testament. I am a good man. I love everybody, including children. I teach people about God."

Megan guessed that it was Moses.

"No, but you're right that he's someone from the Bible." Mom gave us some more clues. "I was born in a barn. I never had a house to live in. I had 12 special friends who followed me around trying to learn all about me."

I tried to answer. "Paul?"

"No, that's a good guess, Topher, but it's not right. This person loved to tell about Heaven. He did miracles."

"Jesus!" Bobbie shouted again. I pretended to plug my ears.

"Bobbie, you're right!" Mom smiled at Bobbie. Bobbie was sitting in the front seat.

And Bobbie smiled a big smile too. I think she was proud for guessing the right answer. "Mom, what was Jesus like?"

"Well, He came to earth as a baby to Joseph and Mary. He grew up like you, but He didn't sin—not even when He was a child. He probably worked with Joseph in the carpenter shop, making things from wood. When He became a man and started the work that His Heavenly Father gave Him, He began doing miracles and talking to crowds of people about God and Heaven."

"Did He talk to children?"

"Oh, yes. He liked children very much. The Bible tells us that Jesus let a child sit on His lap. He told the disciples to let the children come to Him. Parents wanted Jesus to bless their children."

"What's 'bless'?"

"It's when Jesus put His hand on the children's heads and said kind words to them. Jesus would ask God to watch over the children and make them happy. To bless someone is to give kindness, praise or goodness to him."

"I want to visit Jesus someday."

"If you believe He died for you, you will, Bobbie."

QUESTIONS TO ASK YOUR CHILD
1. How was Jesus different from you when He was growing up?
2. How do you know Jesus loved children when He was grown up?

How Old Is Jesus?

One Saturday Bobbie asked Mom if her friend Christy could come over to play. Mom said she could.

"Christy didn't used to live here. She used to live near a big lake in New York in the mountains. She said she was three when she lived there. Now she's four. Do people change ages when they move to a new place?"

"Only if it's their birthday. Moving doesn't change their age. Christy had a birthday when she first came here; that's when her age changed."

"Oh." Bobbie looked like she was thinking about that. She went out the door, but then she came right back in again. "Mom, last night we looked at the picture of Mary and Joseph and baby Jesus in my Bible, remember? How old is Jesus now, Mom?"

"Bobbie, Jesus is God's Son. Jesus lived in Heaven with God forever and ever. He helped God make the world. Then He moved to earth and was a baby. We use the word 'eternal' to describe Him."

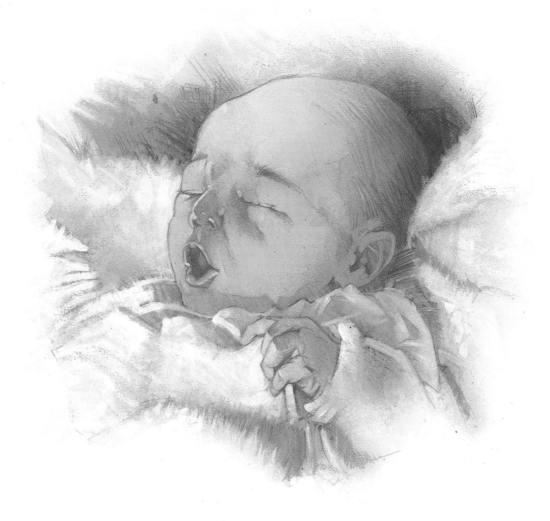

"What's 'eternal'?"
"Well, it means 'no beginning or ending.' "
"So Jesus is so old you couldn't count it?"

"Yes, that's right."

"Then how come He was a baby when He moved to earth? How come He didn't stay forever old?"

"When Jesus came to earth to live, He chose to come as a baby who grew up to be a man."

"How old was Jesus in earth years?"

"He got to be 33 years old, and then He died."

"How old is Daddy?"

"He's 33."

"Is he going to die?" Bobbie looked really scared for a second.

"No, honey. Daddy's healthy."

"But why did Jesus die when He was 33?"

"Because He had finished the job He had come to do. He went back to Heaven."

Verse to Memorize

Hebrews 1:8: "But unto the Son he saith, Thy throne, O God, is for ever and ever. . . ."

QUESTIONS TO ASK YOUR CHILD

1. What does "eternal" mean?
2. How long did Jesus live on earth?
3. Who is eternal?

Where Does Jesus Live?

I have a giant roadway cloth that I lay on the floor, and I drive my trucks and minicars on it. I usually play with it right after supper. Bobbie always wants to play too. I usually let her because it's no fun to play alone. When she plays with me, we pretend that we're going to someone's house and then to someone else's.

Sometimes we say we go to the governor's house. We use special voices. I pretend to knock on the door and ask, "Is this the governor's house?"

Bobbie pretends to be the maid. She likes to say, "By george, the governor does live here."

Then we can go to Uncle Pete's house. We take the long highway and pretend to go to Grandma and Grandpa's. I always want to go to Tommy's house. And Bobbie wants to go to Carrie's house and Melissa's house. We even go to visit famous baseball players like Babe Ruth and Hank Aaron. Of course I know it's all pretend, but I think Bobbie thinks it's real.

Last time I let Bobbie play with me even though I didn't really want to. I was happy when Mom told Bobbie it was time to take a bath and get ready for bed.

"But I can't, Mom. I'm at the governor's house with Toph having tea."

117

"You can, and you will by the time I count to three."

"Yes, Mom." Then Bobbie looked at me. "Governor, I must go home now." Bobbie got up. She tried to take her time, but it didn't work. Mom just put her hand on Bobbie's back and gently helped her. Bobbie started walking toward the hallway.

"Mom, did Jesus ever live in Grafton?"

"No, Bobbie, He didn't."

"Did He ever live in Pennsylvania?" I could hear Bobbie asking questions even when she started going up the stairs.

"No, Bobbie. When Jesus came to earth, He lived with His parents in the town of Nazareth in a country called Israel. It's very far from here, but it's a real place—just like you live with Dad and me in Grafton."

I couldn't find my purple motorcycle, so I went upstairs to look for it in my room. I could still hear Bobbie asking questions.

"Where did Jesus live when He grew up?"

"Well, for most of that time He traveled around, telling people about God. The Bible says He never had a pillow or a place to call His home."

"But where did He sleep and take a bath?"

"Well, Jesus had many friends, like Mary, Martha and Lazarus. Sometimes He stayed with friends, and sometimes He slept outside on the ground under the stars."

"All by Himself?"

"He may have been alone sometimes, but He also had 12 men and sometimes many more who were with Him. He wasn't alone very often."

I found my motorcycle under my bed. I find lots of stuff under there. I took it into Bobbie's room. I kind of wanted to hear what Bobbie was asking.

"Hi, Toph. Mom, after Jesus died and came alive again, where did He live? In that big rock with the angel?"

"No, that was a grave for dead people. Jesus was alive again. He stayed on earth for 40 days, then He left earth."

"Where'd He go? Did He go to the moon or out in space?"

"No, Bobbie, the Bible says Jesus went to be with God in Heaven." I drove my motorcycle on Bobbie's bed and around her dolls' legs.

Bobbie kept talking. "What's Jesus doing in Heaven?"

"Oh, He talks to God about you and me."

"Does He tell God when I'm bad?"

"No, actually He tells God how much He loves you. He's doing something else very important in Heaven."

"What?"

"He's making a place for all those who trust Him and love Him. They will go and live with Him forever."

"Jesus has a place to live in. And all the people who love Him and trust Him get to go there too. I'd like to go to His house. I'll bet it's pretty."

"It is, Bobbie, because God the Father and Jesus are there."

Verse to Memorize

Hebrews 12:2: "Looking unto Jesus the author and finisher of our faith; who . . . endured the cross, despising the shame, and is set down at the right hand of the throne of God."

QUESTIONS TO ASK YOUR CHILD

1. Where is Jesus today?
2. What does Jesus do in Heaven?
3. How can you go to Heaven?

Can I Talk with Jesus?

Every time the phone rings, Bobbie wants to answer it. "I'll get it, Mom! Hello, this is the Schmidt house. How may I help you?" Mom and Dad taught Bobbie how to say that. But she doesn't always answer the phone the right way.

One time Mom was expecting a phone call from Dad. He was working someplace away from home. Mom told us, "If the phone rings this afternoon, don't answer it. I'll get it, you understand?" Megan and I nodded, and Bobbie said, "Yes, Mom."

Tommy came over that day, and we played catch in the backyard. Megan and her friend Ginny were skipping rope. Bobbie kept bugging us. First she wanted to play with Megan and Ginny, but she kept messing up. It was pretty funny. Then she wanted to play with me and Tommy. She did for a while. But she must have got bored, because she went inside.

Bobbie got her shovel and pail to play in the sandbox. She was coming back outside when the phone rang. She ran to get it. I think she thought it was Dad.

"Hello, this is the Schmidt house. How may I help you?" She got it right that time.

But a scary voice said, "I have a collect—" Bobbie didn't even listen to what the man said. She dropped the phone on the floor and ran outside.

After Tommy and Ginny went home, Megan, Bobbie and I went inside. We decided to play Bounce It in the family room. I guess Mom walked by the phone and heard a loud buzzing—you know, that sound the phone makes when it's off the hook. So she came and found us.

"Did any of you children pick up the phone today?"

Bobbie asked, "Why?"

"I just found it off the hook. I wondered why Dad didn't call. That's not like him. He said he would call this afternoon."

Megan and I looked at Bobbie. "Umm, uhh, umm. I picked up the phone when I came in to get a toy. I said 'How may I help you?' like I'm supposed to. But this very scary voice said something, so I just dropped the phone and ran."

"Dropped it and ran? Bobbie, didn't you talk with the person on the phone?"

"No, he was scary! He said something 'bout collect. And I didn't know what to do. I went outside and forgot to tell you."

I could tell Mom wasn't too happy. "Bobbie Lynn, if you can't answer the phone politely, you may not answer it at all. Besides, you disobeyed. I asked you children not to answer the phone today."

"But I wanted to talk to Daddy. I thought it was him. When I heard that other man, I didn't know what to do."

"That's why I asked you not to answer the phone. Dad planned to call collect, and whoever answered the phone needed to accept the charges. That probably was Dad calling."

"It wasn't Daddy's voice."

"No, you heard the operator who
was trying to help Dad make his call.
Since you dropped the phone, Dad
wasn't able to get through. He
must be wondering if we're OK."

Dad called again that night,
but Mom wouldn't let Bobbie
talk with him. It was a
punishment, and Bobbie
cried. "But I love
Daddy, and I wanna
talk to him."

"Bobbie, I know
you love Dad, and
he loves you. He
told me to tell you
that."

"But I wanted to talk
to him myself. I miss him." She kept sniffling.

"Dad's working at a special project where he doesn't have a phone. He has to
make a trip to town to call us. You may talk with him tomorrow when he calls."

"But I want to talk with him now." I wondered if Bobbie would ever stop
crying.

"Next time you should listen better and obey." Finally she did stop and
wiped her nose with her hand. Yuck! Mom didn't like it either so she gave
Bobbie a Kleenex.™

"Mom, does Jesus have a phone in Heaven? Would He ever call collect?
That man sounded like Jesus." I kind of rolled my eyes 'cause I knew Jesus
wouldn't have a scary voice. Bobbie was trying to dis-, dis-, dis—I know the
word. I've heard Mom say it—distrack or something like that. Bobbie was
trying to "distrack" Mom.

"No, dear. Jesus doesn't need a phone."

"Why?"

"Because He and His Father talk with you through the Bible."

"Can I talk to Him?"

"Yes, by praying to Him."

"But I can't hear His voice."

"Yes, but you can talk with Him anytime, even if you don't have a phone. You can talk to God when you're in trouble or when you're happy or when you're alone or when you're with many people. And you don't have to bother with an operator either. You can talk to God the Father through Jesus at any time."

"That's better than a phone. Can I talk to God right now?"

"What will you tell Him?"

"I think I'll tell Him I'm sorry for disobeying you."

"He would like to hear that."

Verse to Memorize

John 15:16: ". . . That whatsoever ye shall ask of the Father in my name, he may give it you."

QUESTIONS TO ASK YOUR CHILD
1. How does Jesus talk to you?
2. How can you talk to God?
3. When should you talk to God?

Does Jesus Have Brothers? Sisters?

Last month at school Megan studied about families. One night we were cleaning off the table after supper when she told Mom she needed help drawing a family tree. It was going to go on the bulletin board at school.

Sometimes Bobbie sits at the table and colors while Megan and I do our homework. I think it makes her feel like a big girl. That night she got off her chair and stood next to Megan. "You're drawing Mom, Dad, Toph and me up in a tree? That's silly."

fire . . . on the Boyces' . . . old barn. . . . I saw . . . Shep down there. . . . Hurry up!"

"A fire at the Boyces' barn? What's Shep doing down there?" Mom was already going out the door. Of course I went too. I had to find Shep.

Megan told us, "He's barking by the back barn door. He won't come when I call him. I'm afraid he's going to go inside."

Mom called Bobbie, and we ran the whole way to the Boyces'. When we got there, I didn't see Shep anywhere. I yelled for him over and over. The fire trucks were there, and lots of people started coming to watch. I walked all the way around the barn. I had to stay pretty far away from it since the fire was very hot. I couldn't get close enough to see inside.

Then I heard Shep barking. It sounded quiet, like he was far away. But I knew it was Shep, and I followed the sound. It wasn't coming from the barn; it was coming from the field. I found Shep lying on the ground with three tiny kittens. He was licking them and trying to clean them up. Shep seemed really tired or something.

He tried to get up when he saw me, but he couldn't. I knew the kittens were the Boyces'. They had just been born last week. I knew 'cause Ginny showed them to me and Megan. The sad thing was that the kittens' mother had been hit by a car and killed. The Boyces fed the kittens with an eyedropper. Shep must have known they were in the barn and gone to rescue them! "Good dog, Shep! Good dog!" I patted him on the head and petted the kittens too.

Then I remembered that Mom would be worried. Whenever I forget that, I get in trouble. So I ran back to tell Mom that I had found Shep. Mom, Megan, Bobbie and I stayed until the firemen finished putting out the fire. The back of the barn was pretty messed up. But Mom said a fireman told Mr. Boyce that he could probably build that part again.

I went back to Shep in the field. Mom brought him some water. I was getting a little afraid because he seemed hurt. He tried to get up but couldn't. "Mom, what's wrong with Shep? Why can't he walk?"

"He may have gotten too close to the flames and smoke. It may have hurt his lungs."

"He'll be OK, won't he?"

"We'll have to wait and see."

Mom went home, but she had Megan bring me my wagon. Megan helped me put Shep into the wagon; then I pulled him home. Mom lifted him out of the wagon and laid him on a huge towel on the back porch.

Bobbie seemed worried too. "Why did Shep get hurt, Mom? Why did he save those kittens?"

"He's a brave dog, Bobbie. He didn't even think about himself; he only wanted to help the kittens."

"But Shep almost died."

"Yes, he is very weak, Bobbie. He was willing to get hurt to save the kittens. They have no mother, and they were too weak to help themselves. Shep is a brave dog."

"Jesus was very brave when He died, right?"

"Yes, braver than Shep because He knew ahead of time the cruel things that were going to happen to Him. And He was so strong that He could have stopped those soldiers. He could have called for ten thousand angels to rescue Him, but He didn't."

Bobbie didn't really get it. "Why would Jesus let the soldiers kill Him, Mom? Did He do something bad?"

"No, nothing. Jesus was perfect. He never did anything wrong. Some men lied about Jesus at His trial."

"Is that the picture in Bobbie's Bible?" I asked that. I remembered seeing it the first day Bobbie got the Bible.

"Yes, it is." Mom smiled at me. But then she looked at Bobbie and Megan. "Jesus died to rescue you."

Bobbie made a goofy face. "But I'm not in a fire!"

"Not now, but if you don't trust Jesus as your Savior by accepting His death for you on the cross, you will face punishment in a place called Hell."

"I don't want to be punished."

"Jesus died so that you wouldn't have to be punished." Mom looked at Bobbie, then Megan, then me. "If any of you would like to tell God you are a sinner and need Him to save you, I want you to feel free to talk to me." Mom smiled and told us again, "Jesus will save you, if you ask Him to."

Verses to Memorize

1 Corinthians 15:3, 4: ". . . that Christ died for our sins according to the scriptures; And that he was buried, and that he rose again the third day according to the scriptures."

John 3:16: "For God so loved the world that he gave his one and only Son, that whoever believes in him shall not perish but have eternal life" (NIV).

QUESTIONS TO ASK YOUR CHILD

1. Why did Jesus die?
2. What happens if you don't ask Jesus to be your Savior?
3. Have you asked Jesus to be your Savior?

Is Jesus Alive Now?

During the summer, our town has Summerfest. It's fun! We play games and ride on this small train. You have to pay to ride a horse or a tractor. People set up booths to sell stuff. Mom calls it "old junk." I guess some of it looks like junk, but some of it is cool. A band plays music most of the time. And all the people walk around, buy junk and eat food. I try to save my allowance for a long time so I have money to spend at Summerfest.

The people from the animal shelter have a booth too. My favorite part of

Summerfest is the animals. Last year they had a cute little black dog with white spots. They had a cocker spaniel with really soft long ears too. They had kittens, but I didn't like them as much as the puppies. And there were tiny rabbits.

I asked my dad probably ten times if I could have a puppy, but he always said, "No, you don't take care of Shep that well. Our family doesn't need another animal for your mother to clean up after."

"But I will take care of it." I told him that, and I meant it! I even promised.

Dad finally said maybe I could get some goldfish. That way, he told me, I could prove myself with a smaller animal. So on our way home from Summerfest, we went to the pet store and bought six goldfish: two for me, two for Bobbie and two for Megan. We bought some fish food and a little fishbowl too.

We named our fish in the car. Mine were Tiger and Spotty. Megan called hers Splish and Splash. Bobbie named hers Whitey and Goldie.

We remembered to feed our fish every day. But after some days, Goldie started looking kind of tired or something. He just hung around the top of the bowl and didn't swim very much. Dad said he was sick. The next day he was floating at the top of the water. Mom had to tell Bobbie that Goldie was dead. Bobbie wasn't sure. "Maybe he'll come back alive again."

"Bobbie, I know it's sad, but Goldie is not alive. He got sick and died. He's not going to get better. We need to get rid of him before he starts smelling up the room."

"We need to wait two more days, Mom. Please!" Bobbie was going to start crying any second. I could tell.

Mom told her the fish would not come back to life. It would not work to wait.

"Yes, it will. I know it."

After two days, we couldn't see inside the fishbowl anymore because the water was so cloudy. I plugged my nose when I got close to it. It stank! And Goldie was still dead. Then Bobbie cried and cried. And she kept saying, "It worked in the Bible. It worked in the Bible."

I tried to figure out what she was talking about. "What do you mean,

Bobbie, 'It worked in the Bible'? Mom didn't read about any goldfish in the Bible."

"When Jesus died, He came alive again after three days."

Mom hugged Bobbie and tried to explain things. "Bobbie, God brought Jesus back to life. It was a miracle. A miracle is a great and mighty work that only God can do. God brought Jesus back to life to prove that Jesus is His Son and that He had forgiven our sins. God wanted us to know that Jesus is also God. Jesus is the only One Who ever came back to life by Himself after He died."

"Oh." Bobbie wasn't crying anymore—at least not as hard. "Maybe God will do it again?"

"Well, Bobbie, Jesus did such a special work that the same event doesn't need to happen again. Because it happened only once, it makes Jesus' coming back alive that much more important. The Bible says that Jesus will come for us and take us to be with Him forever."

QUESTIONS TO ASK YOUR CHILD

1. **What is a miracle?**
2. **Why did God raise Jesus from the dead?**
3. **Is Jesus alive today?**

5
I Have a Question About
SIN

Hints and Helps

Sin. What a negative subject! Our modern world uses euphemisms for sin. The Bible, however, calls sin, sin. Man continually changes his standards concerning sin, but God's standards remain the same.

The Bible pictures sin as primarily the violation of God's law. The main word for sin in the New Testament denotes missing the mark. Romans 3:23 refers to this as falling short of the mark. The Bible also pictures sin as a state of alienation between man and his holy God. The one sin comes from habit; the other sin comes from character. One sin is found in man's actions; the other, in man's very nature. In simple terms, man is sinful, so he sins.

Anyone who has children or is around them for long understands human depravity. Do you have to teach children to resist you or to disobey? From the inside out, children and adults innately know how to sin.

However, part of a small child is unusually pliable and sensitive. The best time to teach children the right way from the wrong way, God's way versus man's way of doing things, is when they are young. You will be surprised at how much young children know about sin. They are keen at picking up on adults' inconsistencies.

The sins of a little child are simple but extremely vivid to him. Who stole the cookies? Who lied to Mom or Dad? Who used bad language? Who lost his temper? Whether it seems small or large, missing the mark is still an affront to a holy God.

Verse to Memorize

    Romans 3:23: "For all have sinned, and come short of the glory of God."

Was Jesus Bad?

Mom sometimes tells me, "Topher, you are a good boy." I know I'm not really that good. While I'm with her and Dad, I usually behave like I'm 'sposed to. But when they're away, sometimes I behave very bad—like one day when Mom thought Tommy and I were collecting newspapers to recycle.

We live kind of close to a horse farm. Out back of the pasture is a creek. Tommy and I like to go swimming there on hot days. Mom usually lets us. But that day she was planning to take Megan to Eastman, and she told me to be home by one o'clock. When Tommy and I got ready to leave in the morning, it was hot already. We were taking my wagon for collecting.

Mom gave me my watch when we left. "Now don't forget to be back in time. And no dipping in the creek this morning."

"OK, Mom." We went to all the other houses on my side of the street, but nobody was home.

"I'm tired of walking. And we aren't getting anything. Let's go to the creek," Tommy said.

I wasn't too sure. "I don't think we better. We have to go to the houses on the other side of the street, and Mom said to be back by one o'clock."

"We don't need to finish the collecting. Let's tell your mom no one was home and just go swimming."

"But that's lying, Tommy!" I really didn't like that idea.

"Your mom doesn't have to know that. Besides, she only cares that you're home on time. We can get back by one o'clock."

"Let's try one more house first."

No one was home at that house either, and Tommy started bugging me again. He teased me and said, "You're too chicken to go swimming, Topher." All boys hate to be called chicken, especially me.

I looked around. "Well, it's sort of true. We tried five houses, and no one was home. All right, but I have to be home by one."

We ran as fast as we could. It wasn't too easy, since I was pulling my wagon. When we got to the creek, we were super hot. Our hair and shirts were all sweaty. We took off our socks and shoes and rolled up our pant legs. The creek water felt great. We splashed each other and played Marco Polo. I closed my eyes, and I had to try to find Tommy by listening to his voice. I didn't know it, but Tommy had climbed out of the creek. When I called "Marco," he was going to say "Polo," but I would never tag him, because I was in the water and he was out of the water!

"Marco," I yelled.

"Po—AH!" Tommy screamed.

I opened my eyes. Tommy was lying on some rocks by the shore. I shouted, "Tommy, are you all right?"

He was crying. I had never seen Tommy cry before. "I think I broke my arm; it hurts—but not too bad unless I touch it." I guess Tommy had fallen on the slippery rocks.

I splashed through the water and over to Tommy. "Let me see," I said. I didn't mean to, but I kind of twisted his arm so I could see it better.

"OW!" Tommy yelled at me.

I put my socks and shoes back on, and I had to put Tommy's on him too. Then he got into the wagon, and I pulled him to my house. It was closer than his.

"Mom, Tommy needs help! He fell."

Mom came out to the porch. "Is it your arm, son?"

"Yes, ma'am." Tommy kind of moaned. Then Mom must have seen Tommy's wet pants and feet. She looked at mine too.

"How did you boys get your pants, socks and shoes all wet?"

I couldn't look at her. "Uhh, walking in the culvert. The water was deep."

"Were you down at the creek?"

"Uhh, no, Mom. We were collecting newspapers."

"Topher, I see weeds caught in your shoes. Those weeds grow only down at the creek. Are you lying to me?"

"No, Mom." I shook my head and tried to look at her. I couldn't do it. "Well, . . . I mean, yes." Then I saw my watch. "We're home on time." I told her. I thought that might make everything OK.

Mom just shook her head. She looked sad. "Let's get Tommy home first, and then you and I will settle this."

"But, Mom, we were early."

"And dishonest and lying and disobedient."

Mom grounded me for the rest of the weekend. I couldn't even go with her, Megan and Bobbie to Eastman. Megan and Bobbie got to buy something at the Everything's a Dollar Store in the mall. And they got drinks at Burger World. That hurt. I felt bad because I had let Mom down. She had trusted me, and I blew it.

When they got home, I told Mom, "I'm sorry I disobeyed you this morning. And I'm sorry I lied to you." Then I asked her if Jesus ever lied to His parents.

"No, He didn't."

"How do you know?"

"The Bible says He was perfect."

"How could a boy be perfect? I didn't want to disobey you. I just wanted to cool off in the creek. Didn't Jesus ever feel like that?"

"No. The Bible is clear that Jesus is God, and when He lived on earth, He never did anything to disobey or break God's law."

"He must have been different from me 'cause I can't help it sometimes."

"Jesus was different from all boys and girls. He was God in flesh, or skin. God is perfect, and so was Jesus—even as a boy."

"I wish I were perfect and did the right thing all the time. Then I wouldn't ever get grounded."

I think Mom liked that idea too because she smiled. "Then I'd never have to ground you." She hugged me, and I knew she'd forgiven me too.

Verses to Read

John 18:38: "... [Pilate] went out again unto the Jews, and saith unto them, I find in him no fault at all."

1 Peter 1:19: "But with the precious blood of Christ, as of a lamb without blemish and without spot."

QUESTIONS TO ASK YOUR CHILD

1. When Jesus was your age, how was He different from you?
2. Did Jesus ever lie to His parents?
3. Name one thing you have a hard time obeying.

Who Goes to Heaven?

Bobbie and Toph were having a little talk. Bobbie kept saying, "Good!" And Toph kept telling her, "Perfect! Bobbie, I'm tellin' you—*perfect!*"

"Good ones! No one is perfect. Mom said so."

"It is too the perfect ones. And that one you're holding isn't one of them." Toph knew he was right. They were sitting in the family room with their baseball cards spread out on the floor.

Mom came into the room. "What are you children arguing about?" Then

Megan came in behind her.

Toph explained about the problem. "Baseball cards, Mom. Bobbie says that we'll get a lot of money for the good ones. I keep telling her only the perfect ones are worth much. Here, look in my book. Sometimes you can get as much as ten dollars for a perfect card. But you only get 25 cents for the good ones that have some small problems."

Bobbie didn't like that. "That's not fair."

"That's why you need my help when you're trading, Bobbie. You don't understand how this works." Toph was trying to be a good big brother, but he couldn't help her if she wouldn't listen to him.

Mom started folding clothes. She had brought a full basket with her. "Your discussion about good and perfect reminds me of how some people feel about who gets to Heaven."

"What do you mean, Mom?" asked Toph. "What do baseball cards have to do with Heaven?"

Bobbie just looked even more confused.

Mom tried to explain. "Many people think that being good is enough."

"Being good isn't enough!" Toph looked at Bobbie when he said that.

"But people can't be very good, can they?" Megan wanted to know. She was helping Mom fold the towels.

Mom shook her head. "When Jesus lived on earth, there was a group of people who were very proud of themselves for living exactly by the Law."

Bobbie asked if they were perfect.

"No, they weren't, even though they tried to make people believe they were."

"I think it's wrong to try and make people believe you're something you're not," Megan said.

"You're right, Megan. That's why Jesus said you would have to live more perfectly than the scribes or Pharisees to enter Heaven."

"Whoa! If that's true, it seems like nobody would ever be good enough." Toph knew he wasn't perfect.

"Me neither. I don't always obey. Do I, Mom?" Bobbie looked at Mom, and Mom shook her head again. Then Bobbie said, "I pray all the time that God

will help me be good, but I keep on doing wrong stuff."

"Well, I can help you with baseball stuff." Toph was trying to be a good big brother again. "But you'll have to get somebody else to help you obey. I'm not even nearly good!"

Mom laughed a little. "You should try to obey. But God doesn't expect us to be perfect before we can get to Heaven. We can't be. That's why He sent Jesus."

Verses to Read

Matthew 5:20: "For I say unto you, That except your righteousness shall exceed the righteousness of the scribes and Pharisees, ye shall in no case enter into the kingdom of heaven."

1 Peter 1:15: "But as he which hath called you is holy, so be ye holy in all manner of conversation [life]."

Romans 3:23: "For all have sinned, and come short of the glory of God."

QUESTIONS TO ASK YOUR CHILD

1. What is God like?
2. What does "holy" mean?
3. How can you be holy?

What Does God Want from Me?

One day at lunch, Mom had a job for Megan. "Mrs. Proper called this morning and wondered if you and Bobbie would take care of her cat while she's gone this weekend."

"I don't know. What do I have to do?" Megan didn't sound too excited.

"She'll tell you. And she's willing to pay you too."

Megan looked like she was thinking for a second. "Well, I guess we could go see her. Come on, Bobbie." Megan and Bobbie went to Mrs. Proper's house next door.

Mrs. Proper opened the door and took the girls into the sitting room. It's really the living room, but Mrs. Proper calls it the sitting room.

She told Megan and Bobbie, "Now girls, my cat is very particular. She likes her food precisely at 8:00 A.M. and 5:00 P.M. Can you handle that?"

"Sure, we can come over after breakfast and before dinner every day." I guess Megan didn't think that would be too hard. And she would get some money.

So Megan and Bobbie fed Mrs. Proper's cat exactly at 8:00 A.M. and 5:00 P.M. on Saturday and Sunday.

On Monday Mom told Megan that Mrs. Proper was home and wanted to see her right away.

"Come on, Bobbie. I'm going to get my money! I'm going to get my money!" Megan sort of sang that, and she skipped out the front door.

A little while later she and Bobbie came back. Megan was walking really slow, and she was looking at her shoes. Bobbie didn't say anything. Mom asked them what was wrong.

"Mrs. Proper wouldn't pay me because she said we didn't give the cat any water." Megan was whining. "But she didn't say to give the cat water! I didn't know. She's so stingy. It's not fair! She only told us to give her food. We were careful and did exactly what Mrs. Proper asked." I could tell Megan was angry!

Mom tried to make things better. "Next time you need to ask her if she has any other instructions before she leaves."

"I'm not going to do anything for her again!" Then Megan looked at Mom. "OK, Mom, I'll try again."

A few weeks later Mrs. Proper was going to her lake cottage for a whole week. She asked Megan and Bobbie to take care of her cat again. That time Megan was trying to be careful. "Please write down what you want me to do so I don't forget anything, Mrs. Proper."

Megan fed the cat at the right times each day. She gave her water and even talked to the cat for a while. She couldn't wait for Mrs. Proper to get home and pay her five dollars. That's how much she had promised.

As soon as Megan saw Mrs. Proper's car in the driveway, she went over there. "Hi! I did everything you wrote down. Could I have my money?"

Mrs. Proper was taking her huge suitcase out of the trunk. "Give me a few minutes to get settled, and I'll call you. You did remember to change the litter box, didn't you?"

"Litter box? You didn't write litter box on your list!" Megan came running home. She was crying.

"What's wrong with you?" Mom stopped Megan as she started to go to her room.

"Now Mrs. Proper made another rule for the cat. Mom, she's not fair. I'm never working for her again! She makes up new rules every time. I think she does it so she doesn't have to pay me!" Mom gave her a hug. Then Mom went to see Mrs. Proper.

Mom came back with four dollars and gave them to Megan. "Mrs. Proper said her whole house smelled when she got home and that you didn't deserve the whole five dollars."

When Megan took the four dollars, she asked, "Mom, does God make up new rules all the time?"

"Why would you ask that?"

"Well, Mrs. Proper seems so perfect, and you said that God is perfect. I wonder if He makes up new rules all the time like Mrs. Proper does."

"Oh, never." Mom sounded sure. "God made up His mind in the beginning. He never changes what is right and wrong. His rules are called commandments."

"Like the Ten Commandments?" Megan asked. Then she said she had heard of them.

Mom nodded. "Yes, those are God's great laws. They're written down for us to know exactly what God expects."

"I'm glad because new rules make things very confusing. And hard."

"I understand how you feel, Megan. But you don't have to feel that way about God's laws. They'll never change, and we have them written down."

Verse to Memorize

James 2:10: "For whosoever shall keep the whole law, and yet offend in one point, he is guilty of all."

Verses to Read

Exodus 20:3–17

These verses record the Ten Commandments of God.

QUESTIONS TO ASK YOUR CHILD

1. Does God ever change what is right or wrong?
2. What does God call His rules?
3. How can you know what is right or wrong?

How Can I Be Perfect?

One day after school I had something exciting to tell Mom. "Mrs. Peters said everyone who has a perfect spelling paper for six weeks in a row will get to go to the big museum downtown. I really want to go!"

Bobbie was sitting at the table coloring again. She asked, "What's perfect, Mom?"

So Mom told her, "It means being right and not making any mistakes."

Bobbie started coloring again. "I'm going to color perfect."

Mom nodded. Then she looked at me. "Will you be able to have six perfect spelling papers, Toph?"

I had just been thinking about that. "I don't know, but I'm going to try really hard."

"Look, I was almost perfect. I only went over the line here and here and here . . . and here and here. Pretty good—right, Mom?"

"Well, that is a good picture. You're doing very well, but you can't be 'almost' perfect, Bobbie."

The next day Bobbie showed us another picture she had colored. "This one's closer perfect," she said. She had gone over the lines only three times.

Mom hugged her and told her she had done a wonderful job. "But remember, Bobbie, perfect means with no mistakes."

The next Friday when I got home, Mom asked me how I did on my spelling test. "I missed two words." I was sad because I wouldn't be able to go on the field trip. "I did much better—why won't that count?"

"Toph, think about God's Ten Commandments."

"The Ten Commandments weren't on our spelling list."

"I mean, think about when God asked His people to obey His ten rules—the ones we read last night in Exodus. God wants us to obey Him all the time."

"I can obey almost perfect sometimes but never perfectly perfect. I keep messing up. Can't Mrs. Peters and God understand we are just people. We can't be perfect!"

"Well, your spelling is better, but it's not perfect yet. Mrs. Peters wants you to do your best. And you know, God is perfect, and Heaven is a perfect place. If God let people who are not perfect into His perfect Heaven, it wouldn't be Heaven anymore. God never changes His mind about sin, Toph. He told us what we need to do."

I think Bobbie finally understood what perfect means. She was listening to Mom and me. Bobbie got really scared. "I'll never make it to Heaven, Mom! I'm not perfect!"

"That's good, Bobbie."

"How can that be good?"

"Because God has a way to make you perfect, Bobbie. God made a way for you in Jesus."

Verses to Read
    Mark 10:17–22

QUESTIONS TO ASK YOUR CHILD

1. What does it mean to be perfect?
2. Can you be perfect?
3. What is God's way for you to be perfect?

Whom Do You Love?

"Christopher loves Melissa. Christopher loves Melissa."

"I do not! And quit calling me Christopher. My name is Toph." Toph doesn't like it when Megan teases him about dumb stuff.

"You do love Melissa. I saw you carrying her books home from school yesterday."

"That doesn't mean I love her. She hurt her arm at recess and needed some help." Toph squinted his eyes and looked at Megan.

But she kept bugging Toph. "Erin lives right next door to Melissa, and you had to walk four extra blocks to help her. Topher loves Melissa."

Then Mom came in. She asked what all the noise was about. So Toph told her, "Megan is telling lies about me."

"It's the truth, not a lie, Mom. Topher does love Melissa."

Mom just said, "You two settle this peacefully, or I'll have to help you."

Toph really doesn't like girls that much. Some girls are his friends. But he doesn't love them. That's mushy stuff.

"But you have to love someone, Toph." Megan pushed further.

"All right, I love Mom and Dad. Are you satisfied?" Toph was starting to get frustrated.

"Do you love Bobbie and me?"

"Stop, Megan! I like Bobbie, and I'm frustrated with you." Then Toph thought of a great way to turn things around. "Megan, who do you love? Billy?"

"Ugh, Billy is weird. I love Mom and Dad and Bobbie and you." Megan seemed serious.

"I saw you give Billy your sandwich at lunch today. You must love him." Toph was teasing Megan, but she ignored him.

Instead of answering Toph, she asked Mom, "Who do you love?"

"Oh I love your dad, you, Toph and Bobbie. I love your grandmas and grandpas. I love my brothers and my sister. I love my friends from church. I love Shep. But I love someone else more than all of you put together."

Megan didn't get that last part because she asked, "How come you love someone more than us, Mom? Who is it?"

"Can you guess Who it is? This person loved me before I ever even knew about Him. He's strong and powerful. He's loving and kind. He's just and holy. This person wants me to love only Him more than I love everyone else."

"I thought you loved Dad the most. You said you'll love him till you die." Megan sounded scared, like she does before she starts crying.

Mom smiled at her. "I will, Megan. But there is still this other person. I have no pictures of Him. I've never seen Him face-to-face. I know a little about Him, but He knows everything about me, and I didn't have to tell Him what He knows. He made a huge sacrifice for me. You know that word, don't you? He gave up something to show His love and to care for a serious problem that I have."

Megan stopped Mom from saying any more. "Mom, tell me who it is! This sounds scary, like you have a secret boyfriend or something."

"No, it's nothing like that." Mom picked up her Bible. "Let me read you something from the Ten Commandments about Who we should love the most. 'I am the LORD your God, who brought you out of the land of Egypt, out of the house of bondage. You shall have no other gods before Me.' The Lord wants our love."

"You're talking about God!" I could tell Megan was happy about that. Then she asked, "Isn't it hard to love someone you can't see?"

"It is different, Megan. But when I remember all that the Bible says God did and does for me, I can't help but love Him. I do have to work at keeping my love for Him greater than my love for anyone else."

"Could I write God a letter and tell Him that I love Him? I'll put in that I'm sorry for teasing Toph." She smiled at him.

QUESTIONS TO ASK YOUR CHILD

1. Who loves you even more than your mom and dad?
2. Whom should you love more than anyone else?
3. Why should you love God the most?

6

I Have a Question About
SALVATION

Helps and Hints

It has to be this way—we must talk about salvation, but only after we talk about sin. We have no need of salvation if we are not sinners. But the Bible is clear; we are sinners. The Bible also clearly teaches that salvation is always by grace through faith plus nothing (Genesis 15:6; Ephesians 2:8, 9).

The question often arises: How soon can children discern their need of salvation? The time-tested rule has always been that if they are old enough to sin, they are old enough to be converted. However, they must have a grocery list; that is, they must have the facts in order to believe. They have to understand that, though their sin offends people such as Mom and Dad and others, sin is primarily and essentially against God's law. Children who are exposed to careful Bible teaching can soon discern the basic facts. However, we should never push children to make a decision for salvation. Neither should we close the door on their decision to follow Christ. Sound Christian teaching containing the basic facts of the gospel (as found in 1 Corinthians 15:3 and 4, for example) is the best way to lead children to salvation.

We should keep in mind that children have tender hearts. The basic rule in gospel work with adults applies to children as well—but on an extremely elementary level. Nonetheless, we should always use the approach that Isaiah used: "Come now, and let us reason together, saith the LORD: though your sins be as scarlet, they shall be as white as snow" (Isaiah 1:18). We appeal to the mind and carefully to the will. Note the two words, "come" and "reason." We should never make any gospel presentation that appeals primarily to the emotions. We should not manipulate the child's will. Whether in the Old Testament or in the New, the basic rule of appeal is always to reason through the Scriptures. Let God turn the will and encourage the heart. Acts 18:4 tells of Paul's work in this regard.

Children are followers and soon become leaders. Beware of the herd instinct in them. Where one goes, others will easily follow without necessarily understanding. So present the gospel, but do not push children for a response. The Holy Spirit will do His work.

For Whom Did Jesus Die?

Our family went on a vacation to Washington, D.C. We stayed a whole week and got to see tons of places. We stayed in Maryland with Uncle Doug. That's not too far from Washington. Every day we went to places to learn about our country. We each liked a different place the best. Megan liked the U.S. Mint. We saw money being made there. It was pretty interesting.

Bobbie said she liked the Washington Monument—especially looking out the windows at the top. You can see almost all of the city if it's a clear day.

From up there we saw the Capitol building, the White House, the Lincoln and Jefferson memorials, the Smithsonian Institution and the Great Reflecting Pool.

My favorite place was the National Air and Space Museum with all the airplanes and other flying machines. I really liked the Space Shuttle because you can walk around in it and check out the buttons.

I think Mom liked visiting the White House and Mount Vernon. She likes the houses of famous people because she likes to see how they decorated.

Dad and Uncle Doug liked the Vietnam Memorial. I thought that was kind of boring. It's just a huge black stone that makes a wall. It starts out very small and gets bigger and bigger till it's higher than Dad's head. I could barely touch the top when I was on Dad's shoulders. And there are names written all over the wall.

I asked Dad, "Whose names are those, Dad? Do you know any of those people?"

"No, I don't, son. I was too young to go to Vietnam, but Uncle Doug knew some of them."

Uncle Doug looked sad. "I sure did, Topher. Some of those people were my friends. I served with them in Vietnam. God protected me, and I came back alive. Not all my friends were that blessed. Look right here at this name. That man was my good friend."

"But why did all those people die, Uncle Doug?" It didn't seem right to me.

Bobbie asked if the people who died were being punished.

Uncle Doug told us, "They died fighting for our country. They died to protect freedom for you and me."

"But, Uncle Doug, I don't even know those men. Why would they die for me?" I didn't quite get it.

"They died fighting an enemy. It was their job."

When we got in the car to leave the Vietnam Memorial, Bobbie asked, "Who did Jesus die for?"

"Yeah," I asked, "was He protecting people too?"

"Bobbie, Toph, those are excellent questions." Uncle Doug is almost as good at answering questions as Grandpa is. "Jesus died for all the people in the world. He died to give people a way to Heaven. His death paid the penalty that we each deserve because of our sin."

"But, Uncle Doug, not everyone knows about Jesus."

"That's true, but it doesn't change what Jesus did or why He did it."

Verses to Read

Isaiah 53:5, 6: "But he was wounded for our transgressions, he was bruised for our iniquities: the chastisement of our peace was upon him, and with his stripes we are healed. All we like sheep have gone astray; we have turned every one to his own way; and the LORD hath laid on him the iniquity of us all."

QUESTIONS TO ASK YOUR CHILD

1. For whom did Jesus die?
2. Why did Jesus have to die?
3. Do you believe Jesus died for you?

How Does Jesus' Death Help Me?

Megan's class at school was having big problems! Someone was stealing other kids' homework. A paper would be gone for two days and then appear again—just like that. Megan's teacher—Mrs. Corrine is her name—said it had to stop. The class had to meet together one afternoon after someone had stolen Megan's math assignment.

"Children, this must stop. We need to find out why someone is stealing homework. We must have a punishment for stealing homework. What do you think would be a fair punishment?"

They talked for a while and finally decided that the person should get a zero for the assignment. They also thought he should go to the principal's office and stay after school for a week.

The next day Megan came in from recess to get her jump rope. She saw Janice in the hallway trying to get something out of Megan's locker. Megan asked her what she was doing, but Megan already knew.

Janice started shaking, and she looked like she was going to cry. "I was putting back your eraser that I borrowed."

Janice has trouble learning things. She has to stay in for recess a lot to finish her papers. Megan likes Janice.

But Janice was holding Megan's math book and her homework paper. Megan's class studies math right after lunch. So Megan figured Janice must have been trying to get her homework done before class. Megan felt terrible for Janice.

She asked Janice, "Why are you holding my math paper?"

"Oh that. I-uhh, uhh, I-uhh. I was putting it back. When I opened your locker to get the eraser, it fell out. I picked it up and was putting it back in your locker for you."

Megan went closer to Janice and talked pretty quietly. "Janice, I don't think that's what happened. Don't steal and lie! Tell me the truth."

Janice did start to cry then. "I can't get it by myself. I can't get math at all! I asked my parents to help me, but all they do is fight. If I get one more zero, I'll flunk math and have to do fifth grade all over again. Please don't tell, Megan. I'm really sorry."

That was a hard decision for Megan. "Janice, I have to tell Mrs. Corrine that you're the one who's been stealing. But I'll tell you what. I can take your zero and stay after school for you. I'll help you with your math if you can come over to my house tonight."

"Why would you do that, Megan? I deserve the punishment, not you. You didn't do anything wrong."

When Megan got home, she told that whole story to Mom. Mom said she was proud of Megan for treating Janice the way she did.

"You know, Megan," Mom told her, "you acted in a way similar to what Jesus did for you."

"What did Jesus do for me? I didn't steal any homework."

"No, you may not have stolen homework, but you—and everyone alive—have done many things to break God's great laws. There always has to be a punishment for wrongdoing. Remember when you lied to me?"

"Oh yeah, I remember. But I told you I was sorry. Isn't that good enough?"

"God says that our sins must be punished. God can't overlook our wrongdoing. The Bible says the punishment for sin is death."

"But I don't want to die!" Megan got a scared look on her face.

"You don't have to if you're willing to admit your sin to God and ask for His forgiveness. Jesus died in your place on the cross just as you took the punishment for Janice."

"But getting a zero and staying after school is nothing like dying for someone. Jesus did that for me? I didn't even know Him."

"Yes, honey, but He knew and loved you."

"I want to ask Him to be my Savior." Megan went with Mom to another room. They talked some more. Then Megan believed on Jesus as her Savior. She got adopted into God's family.

Verse to Memorize

1 Peter 2:24: "Who his own self bare our sins in his own body on the tree, that we, being dead to sins, should live unto righteousness: by whose stripes ye were healed."

QUESTIONS TO ASK YOUR CHILD

1. What must always happen after wrongdoing?
2. According to the Bible, what is the punishment for sin?
3. What did Jesus do for you?

What Does God
Think About Jesus' Death?

"Mom, have you seen my new minicar?" Toph loses those things all the time. Mom usually says the same thing.

"No, Topher. The last time I saw your cars, you were playing with them in the backyard. I haven't seem them today. Ask Megan."

Toph didn't think Megan would have it. But he asked her. "Megan, do you have my minicar?"

"No, Toph, I don't play with cars. You know that. Did Tommy take it home with him on accident?"

He didn't think Tommy had it, so he went to see Dad in the garage. "Dad, did I leave my new minicar out here? I can't find it."

"No, son, I haven't seen it out here. Have you checked your room?"

Toph was getting tired of looking. "Yes, two times. I just can't find the car anywhere. Maybe Bobbie knows where it is." When she came, Toph asked her if she'd seen the car.

And she said, "I buried it in the sandbox for hidden treasure."

"You buried it? Mom!" Toph ran back to the kitchen. "Mom, Bobbie buried my new minicar!" Mom talked to him for a minute; then she called Bobbie. The phone rang, and Mom went to answer it. Toph didn't want to wait till she came back to talk to Bobbie.

"You shouldn't have buried my car, Bobbie! Sand will ruin the gears. I told you not to mess with my stuff unless you ask!"

She only looked a little bit sorry. "Toph, you can go dig it up. I forgot where I buried it though. Sorry."

"Bobbie, sorry isn't enough."

Bobbie looked sort of surprised. "I didn't think you would care."

"Well I do care. I care a lot. That car cost me three weeks' allowance. I only had it one day, and you ruined it! You're going to pay this time, Bobbie Lynn Schmidt."

"How?"

"You're going to find my car! I'll help you look. But if we can't find it, or if I can't get the sand out of the gears, you're going to buy me another one with your own money."

Then Bobbie looked sad. She shouldn't have been sad. "That's not fair. I'm telling Mom, Topher. You're being too mean."

Toph thought he was right. So he told her, "Go ahead. I already asked her. Bobbie, you've done this before!"

Bobbie and Toph dug in the sandbox for an hour. They couldn't find the minicar. Bobbie kept saying, "I know I buried it here. But I'm tired of looking. Sorry, Toph."

Toph wasn't too angry anymore, but Bobbie had to learn her lesson. "No, Bobbie, you're not giving up. You need to learn to be responsible for what you

do." They kept looking.

At lunchtime Bobbie was crying, and they still hadn't found the minicar. Bobbie went crying to Mom, but Mom wouldn't let her get out of her trouble.

After lunch Mom took Bobbie to the store and helped her pick out a car just like the one she had buried in the sandbox.

When they got home, Bobbie gave Toph the new car. "There, Topher. Are you happy now?" She was pouting.

"Yes, I am. Thank you. And next time remember not to take my stuff without asking me."

Bobbie went to tell on Toph. "Mom, Topher wasn't fair to me."

"Actually, Bobbie, he was right to be angry with you."

"But I said I was sorry, and he wouldn't take it."

Mom had to explain to her, "Sometimes being sorry isn't enough to cover a wrong."

"But Toph was mad until I paid him back." Bobbie still didn't get it.

So Mom told her, "Bobbie, it's like Jesus' paying for your sin. God is angry with our sin, and just saying sorry isn't enough. God wants payment for our wrongs."

Bobbie knew what "payment" means, because Megan had explained it to her before. It means when someone pays for something. "What kind of payment does God want? I don't have very much money left."

"God is looking for a blood payment. He wants a life to be given to cover the sin."

Blood payment? Toph frowned at Mom. "Do you mean He wants someone to die?! God must be very upset about sin to want someone to die! Will He ever get unangry?"

"Actually, when Jesus died on the cross and gave His blood for your sin and my sin, God was satisfied with the payment."

Toph asked, "So God is happy with me now?"

"Well, it all depends."

"On what?"

Mom said, "It depends on whether you have admitted to God that you have done something wrong against Him and if you have accepted Jesus' blood payment for you. Some people are too proud to admit they're wrong. They insist on trying to pay their own payment for sin."

"God won't take their payment, right?" Toph wanted to make sure he understood the whole thing.

"That's right."

"They must be silly, Mom." Bobbie had been listening the whole time. "I don't want God to be angry at me. I'll trust Jesus to pay for my sin."

Verse to Memorize

   1 John 4:10: "Herein is love, not that we loved God, but that he loved us, and sent his Son to be the propitiation for our sins."

QUESTIONS TO ASK YOUR CHILD
1. How does Jesus feel about your sin? 2. How did Jesus take care of your sin? 3. How can God be pleased with you?

How Do I Get
the Free Gift?

The commercial said, "Free." But it seemed too good to be true. Mom thought so too. "It does sound too good to be true, Toph. There must be a catch."

Dad didn't even think we should go. "We Schmidts never take anything for nothing. We work for what we get."

But I sure wanted a new baseball glove! The commercial said the sports stadium was giving them away—FREE—to the first 50 fans in the door on Thursday.

"Dad, please will you take me to the ballpark and check it out? Please?"

"All right, son, but don't expect to come home with a new ball glove. There's no such thing as a free lunch, you know."

I don't always know what Dad means when he says stuff like that. I told him, "I want a free glove, not a free lunch." I was just glad we were going.

We went to the ballpark a whole hour early. I thought for sure we would be the first people there. But when Dad turned the last corner, I couldn't believe it! The cars already stretched as far as I could see. I guess everyone in town had heard about the free offer.

We parked the car and got in line anyway. I knew we were too far back to be in the first 50. I tried counting the people in front of us. But they kept moving, and I couldn't get past 25. Tommy came with his dad, but they were really far back.

Finally the gate opened, and people started going in. I guess the ball gloves were only for boys who were eight to ten. I hadn't heard that part in the TV commercial. Maybe they didn't say it. Or maybe they only showed the words or something.

Anyway, it turned out that I was the 49th boy in line who was eight, nine or ten years old. I was so happy! Tommy was number 60 though, and he didn't get anything.

When we got home, I told Mom, Megan and Bobbie. Mom even let me call Grandpa and Grandma Williams to tell them.

Grandpa said something different when I told him about the glove. "Kind of reminds me of salvation."

"What do you mean, Grandpa?"

He told me, "God offers salvation as a free gift. Some people think it's too good to be true and never act upon it. Some people are skeptical like I was and hesitate to check it out. Then there are people like you, Toph, full of trust and hope. They keep looking until they find. God's gift is free, but we must act to receive it. Jesus paid the price, but a person must respond and receive it for himself."

"Remember when I trusted Jesus as my Savior at your house last summer? I'm glad I did."

Verses to Memorize

Ephesians 2:8, 9: "For by grace are ye saved through faith; and that not of yourselves: it is the gift of God: Not of works, lest any man should boast."

QUESTIONS TO ASK YOUR CHILD

1. What is God's free gift?
2. How can you receive the free gift?
3. Have you accepted God's gift of salvation?

I Sinned Again, Now What?

"Mom, can I have a sheet of paper?" Bobbie is always asking Mom for paper to color on.

"Sure, Bobbie, what are you drawing?"

"A special picture for you and Dad. I can't tell you."

Mom was working on some crafts at the kitchen table, while Bobbie colored. A while later, Bobbie asked, "Mom, can I have another sheet of clean paper?"

"Yes, Bobbie." Mom gave her a sheet. "How are you coming on your picture?"

179

"Not too good. I keep messing up. Maybe you can give me five more sheets."

"No, Bobbie, work with what you have for now, and if you need more, I'll give it to you. I don't mind your asking. I like to have you talk to me. Besides, it helps me to know how you're coming along with your work." Then Mom and Bobbie worked on their projects and talked about different stuff.

It wasn't too long until Bobbie messed up again. "Mom, do you have another sheet of paper for me?"

"Yes, but let's talk about why you keep messing up. Are you making the same mistake every time? Is there some way I could help you?"

Bobbie showed Mom her messed-up papers. "Yes. I'm trying to draw a house like ours, and I can't do it right. Can you draw one for me to copy?" So Mom drew a house, and Bobbie copied and

colored it. When Megan and I came into the kitchen, Bobbie showed us the picture. It was pretty good.

Bobbie gave the paper to Mom, and Mom hugged her. "It's for you, Mom. I finally got it right. Thanks for helping me. Thanks for giving me new paper when I messed up."

"You're welcome, honey." Mom hung Bobbie's picture on the refrigerator.

Then Megan asked, "What did you mess up?" And Bobbie told us what had happened.

I told Bobbie the house looked good. But Megan must have been thinking about something else. She asked, "Mom, how does God feel when we keep messing up? You know, keep sinning? Does He ever get angry and throw us out of His family?"

"No, Megan, the Bible says that God is long-suffering."

"What's 'long-suffering' mean?"

"It means that He sticks with us a very long time. He keeps forgiving and forgiving."

I guess Megan still wasn't sure about that. "Does God ever say, 'That's enough,' and give up on us?" she asked.

"The Bible says that if we do wrong all the time, we're probably not God's children. If we were really born into God's family, we would not continually sin. Every time we tell God our sins, God forgives us. The Bible says He is 'faithful . . . to forgive.' But we must do our part."

"What's our part, Mom?" Megan was asking all these questions.

"It's obeying God and His Word and confessing our sins to Him when we disobey. 'Confessing' means telling God what we did wrong. God changes our hearts when we are born into His family. Then what we do should change too. God gives us a special new heart attitude, and He changes our mind about sin to help us."

Megan nodded, so I guess it made sense to her. "Mom, you were sort of being like God when you helped Bobbie every time she messed up."

Mom just nodded and smiled.

Bobbie gave Mom another hug. They hug a lot. "Mom, thanks for helping me over and over like God. I love you."

Verse to Memorize

1 *John 1:9:* "If we confess our sins, he is faithful and just to forgive us our sins, and to cleanse us from all unrighteousness."

```
┌─────────────────────────────────────┐
│     QUESTIONS TO ASK YOUR CHILD      │
└─────────────────────────────────────┘
```

1. How is God long-suffering to you?
2. What does the Bible say about a person who sins all the time?
3. If you are saved, what are you to do when you sin?

How Long Do You Stay in God's Family?

Whenever we're at Grandpa and Grandma's, Bobbie likes to go on walks with Grandpa. One day when we were there, some sheep got out of the fence and went over to the neighbor's field. They started eating his crops! Farmer Peet called and asked Grandpa to come and get the sheep.

"Can I go too, Grandpa?" Bobbie loved to go with Grandpa and see the sheep. "I could help you to call them and bring them back home."

"Well, you can't really help call them, Bobbie. But you're welcome to come along for the ride." Grandpa went with Bobbie out the back door.

As they walked to the truck, Bobbie told Grandpa that she can call really loud. I showed her how. But she had forgotten one thing. "What words do you say to the sheep, Grandpa?" she asked.

"When I want them to come to me, I say, 'Here, nanny, nanny.'"

When Bobbie and Grandpa got to Farmer Peet's, they walked over to the sheep. Grandpa nodded at Bobbie. "Go ahead and try, Bobbie."

So Bobbie called. She did the best job she could, but the sheep wouldn't come. They wouldn't even look at her! She tried and tried and tried. She made her voice louder and louder. She made it sound different too, but the sheep didn't move until Grandpa called in a pretty quiet voice, "Here, nanny. Here, nanny, nanny."

Then—right away—the sheep looked at Grandpa. They stopped eating and went straight back to the hole in Farmer Peet's fence, where they had gotten in. They crossed the road and looked for the opening in Grandpa's fence. They went back in at exactly the same place they had come out.

I think Bobbie was disappointed with the sheep. She reached up to hold Grandpa's hand. "Grandpa, why didn't the sheep listen to me?" she asked. "I called and called, and they wouldn't listen."

"They know my voice, and they respond to their owner. Sheep are like that, Bobbie. And so are people."

"You don't say 'Here, nanny, nanny' to people, Grandpa."

"No, but the Bible says that people are like sheep, and they know the voice of their owner."

"Who's our owner, Grandpa?"

"Why, God is."

"God and Jesus are eternal life, right, Grandpa?" Bobbie was almost right.

Grandpa told her, "God and Jesus are eternal. Eternal life is also called everlasting life. It means life that has just a beginning but no ending. It goes on and on forever."

"Are people bad sheep sometimes? Will God give His sheep to someone else?"

"I'm sure our sin makes God displeased, but—"

"What does 'displeased' mean?" Bobbie interrupts people when she doesn't know a word.

"It means unhappy or upset. Even when our sin displeases God, He promises never to let us go. He holds on to us and won't let anything take us out of His strong hand." He looked at his big hand holding Bobbie's little one.

"You have strong hands too, Grandpa."

Grandpa squeezed her hand a little bit. "Can you help me fix the fence so these sheep don't get out again?"

"Yes." Bobbie smiled at Grandpa. "Thank you for holding my hand."

Verses to Memorize

John 10:27, 28: "My sheep hear my voice, and I know them, and they follow me: And I give unto them eternal life; and they shall never perish, neither shall any man pluck them out of my hand."

QUESTIONS TO ASK YOUR CHILD
1. How are people like sheep?
2. What does God give to those who follow Him?
3. Does God ever give His children away?

7

I Have a Question About
CHURCH

Helps and Hints

Some baby boomers left the church in their earlier years for what they believed were more important pursuits. Now some of those baby boomers have children, and they are rediscovering the church to help them answer their children's questions.

Some Christians don't think much of the local church. These people gather in all kinds of Christian groups outside the church, but seldom are they loyal to a local church. They are something like the world traveler who never got to know his own family.

When we speak of church, we might refer to the "universal church," which includes all the people (from Acts 2 until the coming Rapture) who have confessed their sins and embraced Christ as Savior. Although the universal church is real, we cannot see it. If I am hurt, I cannot go to the universal church for consolation. If I need counsel, I can't speak with the pastor of the church universal, as there is no such person. Thus "church" primarily refers to a local body of believers, of which we all need to be a part. The local church exists to meet our spiritual needs, as well as the needs of all the other members.

We sometimes say that God ordained three institutions. The first is the family. God loves families; therefore, He started the whole race with a family. Then after Adam sinned, God created human government, or the principle of human authority over us. Paul wrote about government and authority in

Megan was acting really smart that day. School had gotten out just a few days before, and she had won an award for being the best student in her class.

Mom was trying to remember the buildings they had just passed. "Do you mean the museum?" she asked Bobbie.

"No, the fancy one with the poi—spike! Sometimes the spikes have sticks on top, but sometimes they don't. Sometimes they have windows, and sometimes they don't have windows." Bobbie was trying to explain the buildings, but it wasn't helping Mom. "There's another one, Mom, right there." Bobbie pointed out the window again.

Mom couldn't look that time. "Bobbie, I want to answer your question, but you keep waiting until we've passed the building before you point it out to me. Remember that I'm driving and need to look out the front window to keep the car moving safely."

Bobbie kept staring out the window. She pointed out the next pointy thing sooner. "There's another one, Mom. What's that spike thing?"

Mom finally saw one. "Oh, that's a church steeple. It's tall and white and points to the sky to remind people that God is much greater, higher and holier than we. The sticks are actually a cross. Some churches have a cross there to remind people that Jesus died on the cross to pay for our sins. The windows are just to make it pretty."

"Does a church have to have a steekle?"

"It's 'steeple,' not 'steekle,' Bobbie. And many churches don't have steeples. Some churches don't even have buildings. In parts of Africa and South America, people love God and belong to His church without having a building of any kind. Some places have warm weather all year, so buildings aren't as important there. The people who love God just have a special meeting time when they all get together. It's fine to have a fancy building to remind us how beautiful and big God is, but that doesn't make a church. People do. You only have to have people who love God and have asked Jesus to save them from their sins to have a church."

The children were quiet for two whole blocks. That's a long time for them. Then Megan asked, "Does everyone at church love God? What about the people who don't know about Him but want to learn?"

"Anyone is welcome to go to church—the building or the meeting. Church is a great place to learn about God. In fact, many people who just visit eventually decide to be in God's family."

That night at dinner, Dad asked what the children had done that day. He asks them that all the time. Megan told him about the talk they had had about spikes and churches and God's family.

Then Bobbie asked some questions. "Dad, are you in that family? Am I in the family? Am I the church?"

"Bobbie, I'll have to think about that and answer you later. I have been thinking about some of those things for a while now. Maybe it's time to make up my mind. I think maybe we'll visit the 'spike place' this Sunday."

Verse to Read

Acts 2:47b: "And the Lord added to the church daily such as should be saved."

QUESTIONS TO ASK YOUR CHILD
1. Why do steeples point to the sky?
2. What is a church?
3. Are you a part of the church?

Who Is the Man Standing Behind the Box up Front?

Bobbie woke up early! The night before she had gotten out her best dress, her good shoes and her socks that have lace on them. She got dressed and tiptoed into Mom and Dad's room. "Dad, is it time to go yet?"

"Bobbie, it's only 5:30! We don't have to get up till seven. Please go back to bed. I'll make sure you're up in time."

Bobbie went back to her room and took off her fancy clothes. She was quiet. But she was excited because they were going to visit the church with the spike.

After Dad had gotten Toph up, he went to Bobbie's room and told her it was time to get going. Bobbie practically jumped out of bed. She even beat Toph getting ready. She brought her Bible to the kitchen for breakfast.

When Bobbie, Megan, Mom and Dad and Toph were in the car on their way to the church, Bobbie stared out the window. Then she yelled, "There's the spike!" when she saw it from blocks away, above the treetops.

Megan had to tell her the right word. "Bobbie, it's a steeple. And please try to keep your questions to yourself today." Megan told Toph she was afraid Bobbie would say something dumb in front of everybody at the church.

Two men shook their hands when they walked into the church. The men seemed pretty nice. They said, "Hello! Thank you for coming!" One of them pointed the family to a big room with long wooden seats with ends on them. Mom said they're called pews. The man even helped them find a place to sit. The room was kind of pretty if you like fancy lights and colored windows.

Bobbie had to sit between Mom and Dad. "Mom, there's a piano like Megan plays." Then she crawled onto Dad's lap. "Dad, what's that big box up there?"

Megan was embarrassed. "Shhh, Bobbie. This is church, and you're supposed to be quiet!"

Dad told Megan he would take care of things. Then he answered Bobbie's question. "That's an organ. It plays beautiful music."

"Why?"

"Well . . . umm . . . the music helps you think about how big and mighty God really is. Listen, the lady is beginning to play the organ."

All the people in the church got really quiet when the lady played the organ. And everyone stayed quiet when she was done. Everyone except Bobbie. She got off Dad's lap and got onto Mom's. In a super loud whisper, she asked, "Mom, who's that man behind the box up front? What's he doing with the big book?" Toph looked at Megan and rolled his eyes. Megan slid down in the seat. But Mom and Dad seemed happy that Bobbie wanted to know what was going on.

Mom told her that it was the pastor. "He has the Bible with him. He'll read it out loud later this morning. The pastor is the leader of the church.

Sometimes he's called a shepherd. I'll tell you more when we get home. Let's listen now, OK?"

Bobbie seemed to love church. The organ music was beautiful like Dad said. She liked the people up front who sang a special song. She really liked the sheep herder man that Mom said they would talk about later.

After a while a man said, "We'll dismiss the children at this time." A bunch of kids got up and started to leave. Dad whispered to Toph that he and Megan and Bobbie could go with the other kids, so they followed them to a big room downstairs.

Bobbie went to one place for children. Megan and Toph went to a different church for older kids.

When they got home Dad read from the Bible. He was reading from a place called First Peter, chapter 5. It was something to do about Christ, Who is the big Shepherd, and about the pastor of the church, who is the little shepherd.

Bobbie shook her head. "The man behind the big box at church was really tall. How come the Bible calls him a little shepherd?"

"It doesn't mean size. It means that Jesus Christ is the head, or the leader, of the church. The pastor is under Him."

Mom tried to help Dad explain it. She said, "The pastor reminds me of what my dad, your Grandpa Williams, does."

"Grandpa doesn't stand behind a big box and talk."

"No, but he does feed his sheep every day. He finds the best water for them and helps them when they get into trouble. In the same way the pastor of the church feeds the people good food from the Bible to help them grow to love God more and obey Him better. When the people get into trouble, he tries to help them with wise ways from the Bible. He knows that book very well."

"The people at church are sheep?" It sounded funny when Bobbie said that, but she was kind of right.

Mom told her, "Well, Bobbie, they behave like sheep and need lots of help. I'm glad that church has a good pastor."

Dad had been really quiet while Mom was talking about Grandpa and sheep. But then he said, "I think it's time I talk with that pastor about becoming a member of the church."

Bobbie asked him, "Dad, are you going to be a sheep? Will you eat grass?" That sounded even funnier.

But Dad didn't laugh. He just said, "No, Bobbie, but I'm going to talk with the shepherd and find out what I need to do to be under God's care."

Verses to Read

1 Peter 5:1–4: "The elders [pastors] which are among you I exhort, who am also an elder; . . . Feed the flock of God which is among you, taking the oversight [of it], not by constraint, but willingly; not for filthy lucre [money received dishonestly], but of a ready mind; neither as being lords over God's heritage, but being [examples] to the flock. And when the chief Shepherd shall appear, ye shall receive a crown of glory that fadeth not away."

QUESTIONS TO ASK YOUR CHILD

1. Who is the head of the church?
2. Who is like a shepherd at church?
3. What should a pastor do?

Why Does Our Family Get Together?

Mom was kind of crabby like she always is when company is coming. She had a list on the refrigerator that had at least 25 "Things to Do." She told us to sign up for "five jobs each" and to have them done by lunch the next day. I knew I would be glad when our cousins finally got here. Getting ready for company isn't much fun.

Dad and I decided to take the outside jobs so that we could work together and be out of the house. We said we would mow the lawn, sweep the back porch and pick up branches that had blown down in the windstorm the night before. Those are the boy jobs. We let the girls do the girl jobs inside—like cleaning out closets and drawers and straightening the canning jars in the basement.

I love to ride with Dad on the riding mower. It's so much fun, and it counts as work. We were halfway through mowing the backyard when Bobbie came out of the house crying. It was more fake crying than real crying. I think Bobbie does that when she wants something.

Bobbie sat down on the back porch and put her head down. Dad stopped the mower, and I went over to see if I could help.

"Bobbie, what's wrong?" I asked it as nice as I could.

"I hate company! I wish our cousins wouldn't even come!" She sure was crabby!

"Why? You've been driving us all crazy saying you can't wait until our cousins get here. Why'd you change your mind?" I was trying to be a kind big brother.

"I can't stand getting ready for them to come! I was picking up my toys and taking them to my room. My toy box was full, so I put my other toys under my bed. No one looks there but Mom." Bobbie was talking in a whiny voice.

"Let me guess. Mom came to check your work and found the toys under the bed. And she made you put them away all over again."

"How did you know?"

"I used to do that too when I was your age. I always got caught. Don't worry, Bobbie. Our cousins will be here before dinner tonight."

"Topher, why does our family have to get together anyway? It's too much work!"

"The cousins are coming to spend their vacation with us. I guess it's 'cause we love each other. Getting ready is kind of a pain, but it's fun when they're here. I can't wait until Trent gets here so I'll have another boy to play with. We had a blast last year when we went to their house in Atlanta for a week. They prob'ly have to get ready for us before we go there too. Anyhow, just keep thinking about how much fun it will be when they get here." Megan came out of the house too. She sat next to Bobbie.

Bobbie still seemed crabby. She told me, "Mom said we're going to their house for Christmas this year. And she said we're going again in the summer. Why do we get together so much?"

I tried to make Bobbie laugh. "Just think, they have to do the cleaning twice in a row." She finally smiled.

Then Megan answered her question. "We get together because we love each other and want to have fun together. I guess it's kind of like that new church we visited last week. I think they must have worked hard getting ready for us to visit. They seemed like they really loved God and were happy to have visitors."

I was thinking about the church teacher. "She told us a story from the Bible, and she gave us a word puzzle to do. We had snacks and played a game and sang songs. She must have worked hard to find all that stuff to do."

Bobbie was finally not acting crabby. She smiled and said, "I'll bet God is glad when we come to visit at His house because He doesn't have to do any of the work to get ready!"

Megan nodded, but she had a funny, faraway look on her face—like her brain was far, far away. "Those people sure do seem to love God. They love Him so much that they keep His house clean and beautiful—"

"—While He's somewhere else!" Bobbie finished Megan's sentence for her.

Then I said, "I think they must love God more than we love our cousins."

Bobbie jumped up really fast. "I better finish helping Mom get ready!"

Verse to Read

Hebrews 10:25: "Not forsaking the assembling of ourselves together, as the manner of some is; but exhorting one another: and so much the more, as ye see the day approaching."

QUESTIONS TO ASK YOUR CHILD

1. **What is one way you can show God you love Him?**
2. **Why do people get together?**
3. **How often do you go to church to show Jesus you love Him?**

Does God Get His Children Together?

"Bobbie, you must go to bed early tonight. You have 10 minutes to finish building your tower." When Mom said that, she set the timer. "When the timer goes off, I want you to head for the bathroom. I'll have your bath ready for you."

"Mom! I'm not tired!" Bobbie whined. She sure sounded tired.

Mom did not sound happy. "Bobbie, you were up hours past your bedtime every night for a week while your cousins were here. You've been fussy and crabby all day, and you will go to bed early tonight. Enjoy your 10 minutes, or we can begin the bath right away. Understand?"

"Yes, Mom." Finally Bobbie knew she wouldn't win. She finished her tower and actually picked up all the blocks before the timer dinged.

During her bath she asked Mom some of her famous questions. "Mom, does God ever have all of His family get together like we do?"

"What do you mean, Bobbie?" Mom asked her.

"Does God get His family together at Christmas or vacations? You said that God has a family with lots of children. Who cleans up before they get together?" Bobbie was still remembering when her family had to clean for the cousins.

Mom told her, "God's family today is called the church. And God does want them to get together often. Today people meet together at least once or twice a week. In the Bible the church met every day and ate together every day. The people were so glad to be in God's family. They met in different homes and shared food. They also had a special meal of eating bread and drinking grape juice like Jesus did the last time He ate with His disciples. The church people were the happiest people you could ever see. They loved God so much, and they liked being with each other. They got along and didn't fight at all."

"What a nice family! But who cleaned up for the guests coming? Did God have to go to bed early so He wouldn't be crabby?"

Mom answered her first question. "Actually each family probably cleaned up their home when the gathering was at their place. The believers—that's another name for them—were like one big happy family." Then Mom laughed a little. "To answer your other question, young lady—God is perfect, so He never gets crabby and doesn't need His rest like you and I do. Actually, Bobbie, thousands of people came into God's family every day at the beginning."

"Is that like zillions?"

"Well, it is more people who love God than I've ever seen in one place."

"Does God come to the parties? If all the people are in His family, does He ever come to see them? Or does He stay in Heaven and watch on TV what they're doing?"

"God sent His Son Jesus to earth for 33 years to live with people, die and

come alive again. He did all that so people would trust Him as Savior and be a part of His family. He can see everything that happens on the earth at once because He's everywhere at the same time. God doesn't need a TV screen to know what's going on."

"Why don't we meet every day with God's family like they did in those old days?"

Mom gave a really big sigh. "Oh, Bobbie. Save that question till later. It's time to finish up the bath and head for bed."

206

Verses to Read

Acts 2:41, 42, 46: "Then they that gladly received his word were baptized: and the same day there were added unto them about three thousand souls. And they continued stedfastly in the apostles' doctrine and fellowship, and in breaking of bread, and in prayers. . . . And they, continuing daily with one accord in the temple, and breaking bread from house to house, did eat their meat with gladness and singleness of heart, praising God and having favour with all the people. And the Lord added to the church daily such as should be saved."

QUESTIONS TO ASK YOUR CHILD

1. What is the family of God called?
2. How often does God want His family to get together?
3. Why doesn't God come to the gatherings Himself?

Why Do People Get Wet in Church?

"Please, please, please, please, can't I go too? I want to go with you to church to see the pastor." Bobbie hugged Dad's legs when he was getting his car keys and Bible. "I wanna go with you when you talk with the shepherd man. I like his voice. Please, please, please, please, can't I go with you?"

Dad thought about it for a second. But then he said OK. "But you'll have to be on your best behavior. Is that possible? This is a very important meeting. I have important questions of my own to ask Pastor, and I can't be interrupted

by your questions. It's fine for you to ask questions, but right now I need to get some answers myself. What do you think?" Dad sounded like he meant it.

But Bobbie really wanted to go. "I'll be very good. I can go in the big room and sit still while you talk with Pastor. Please, Dad?"

Dad peeled Bobbie off his legs. "OK. Get your shoes on, and let's go. I'm supposed to be there in five minutes."

When they got to church, Dad took Bobbie to the big room with the piano and organ. It's called the auditorium. Dad told Bobbie to wait for him there. She saw Dad and Pastor walk into a room down the hall. Then she went inside the auditorium. It looked super big without any people in it. She sat down and pulled a songbook from the rack. Then she pretended to sing a song. She does that at home too. She's so silly.

Splish-splash! Bobbie heard a funny noise coming from the front of the room. She slid down low in the seat so no one could see her. It sounded like water running really fast. And she heard a man singing.

Bobbie peeked over the edge of the seat. She saw a man standing behind the box that Pastor talks from. Then he turned and stuck his head in a big window-thing in the wall. He was wearing work clothes, and he seemed to be very busy working with the water. Bobbie was a little scared, so she got up and tiptoed out of the room. She sat on a chair outside the door where she had seen Dad go in with Pastor. And just a minute later Dad and Pastor came out of the room and shook hands.

On the way home, Bobbie asked Dad about the man. "Dad, was that man getting ready to take a bath?"

Dad smiled at that question. "That was the janitor, Bobbie. He was checking the baptistery so it will be ready for me."

"For you? But we have a bathtub at home. You can take a bath there."

Then Dad tried to explain. "Bobbie, it's not a bathtub, although it does hold water in it. It's a tank used in church services when people want to tell others that they are followers of Jesus. It's like a ballplayer wearing a uniform that tells other people which team he plays for. That's what I wanted to talk to Pastor about today. I have decided to admit that I need Jesus as my Savior. I did that today with Pastor while you were in the auditorium. On Sunday I'm going to be baptized to tell everyone that I'm a follower of Jesus. That man was getting the tank ready for me."

"So it's for telling people that you love Jesus? How come you can't just say it? Why do you have to get all wet in church, Dad? Will you wear your swimming suit?"

"Whoa, little girl. One question at a time. The Bible way of telling people that you belong to Jesus is to be baptized, or completely covered with water. Baptism shows how Jesus died, was buried and then came back to life again. When Pastor lowers me into the water, that will show how Jesus was crucified, or that He died. Then when I'm under the water, that will show how Jesus was buried. And when Pastor brings me out of the water, it will show that Jesus came back to life three days after He died and was buried. Does that make sense?"

Bobbie just nodded, so Dad went on. "I'll wear a robe over my clothes. Several others will be baptized at the same time."

"Are some of them children, Dad? Are there other dads or moms? Any grandmas or grandpas?"

"Yes, there are some children being baptized, one other mom and dad, and Mrs. Jenkins. The service will be on Sunday. That's in three days."

Bobbie leaned over and patted Dad's leg. "Dad, I am so happy!"

Verses to Read

Acts 2:41: "Then they that gladly received his word were baptized: and the same day there were added unto them about three thousand souls."

Acts 16:30, 31 and 33: ". . . Sirs, what must I do to be saved? And they said, Believe on the Lord Jesus Christ, and thou shalt be saved, and thy house. . . . And he . . . was baptized, he and all his, [immediately]."

QUESTIONS TO ASK YOUR CHILD

1. What does being baptized tell people?
2. How does baptism show what Jesus did for you?
3. If you are saved, have you been baptized?

Why Do They Sing So Much in Church?

Megan was practicing a song on the piano for the 100th time in one morning. It was an easy song, and it sounded sort of pretty—I guess. Megan was going to play for church on Sunday night, and she wanted to have the song perfect. It was the first time she had ever played in front of that many people. Mom said Megan should do her best for God.

But Bobbie and I got tired of listening to the same song over and over. "Can't you play anything else? I used to like that song, but I can hear it in my sleep." And I was serious! I really wanted her to stop playing that song!

"Turn the page, Megan. I don't like that music anymore. My ears are tired." Bobbie said that a little nicer than I did, but I know she was really sick of the music too. Then Bobbie asked Mom, "Why do we have so much music at church? We sing more than anything else. Does God like music? Does He get tired of hearing us sing?"

"Those are good questions, Bobbie. I'm just not sure how to answer them. Maybe the choir director could help us. Or—I know—let's try to find the answer ourselves."

"How?"

"Get your Bible, and let's look in the back under the concordance for the word 'sing' or 'music.' That way we can find out what the Bible says about making music. I'd like to know too."

"What's a condolence?" Every time Bobbie gets her words mixed up, I laugh at her. I can't help it. It's funny.

"It's 'concordance,' Bobbie, not 'condolence.' A concordance is like an easy way to find where things are. Condolence is help for someone who feels sad."

That sounded good to me. "I need condolence with Megan playing that song so much. Make her stop, Mom, please!"

But Mom was already looking in Bobbie's Bible. "Here it is under 'song.'

The book of Job says, 'Now am I their song. . . .' God is the One we are to sing about. The Bible says that God gives songs in the night. That means He helps us to sing even in times of trouble. The book of Psalms uses the word 'song' a lot. The Bible tells us to sing unto the Lord. So we sing to Him and about Him. It sounds to me like God wants us to sing."

Bobbie didn't say anything for a minute. I think she was listening to Megan play her song—AGAIN—because then she said, "I think God must get tired of the same song over and over again."

Mom smiled at Bobbie and at me. "Well, actually, I think God enjoys even the same song over and over, because He knows the person is singing or playing an instrument for Him. He enjoys when we do our very best. And He likes things to be done right. I guess you'll have to be patient a little longer with Megan and her practicing. Maybe you and Topher can find a song of your own to sing in the basement or out on the porch so your ears can get a little rest."

Verse to Read

Colossians 3:16: "Let the word of Christ dwell in you richly in all wisdom; teaching and admonishing one another in psalms and hymns and spiritual songs, singing with grace in your hearts to the Lord."

QUESTIONS TO ASK YOUR CHILD

1. Can you name one book of the Bible that says you should sing?
2. Who should you sing about?
3. Why should you do your best when you sing?

Why Is Church
So Much like School?

The night Dad was baptized was a big night at our house. Grandma and Grandpa Williams came all the way from Pennsylvania. Megan, Bobbie and I wore our best clothes. Mom seemed sad or happy—I couldn't tell which, because she kept crying.

After the service when Dad and the others got baptized, we went to a place in the back of the church. I had never been in that part of the church before. We walked in a long hallway. Bobbie and I were kind of walking behind everyone else.

Bobbie was looking all around. "This seems like a school. Can I look in this room, Toph?"

"I guess so. But don't take too long, or we'll get lost and never find Mom and Dad."

"Look, Topher! This room has chalkboards and pictures. The chairs and tables are little for kids like me! And there's cans of pencils and crayons. It looks like preschool. Can I go?"

I told her I didn't know. When we went back to the hallway, Bobbie kept talking about it. "I wanna go to school. Mom says I have to wait. I'm going to go to kindergarten when it's school time. But I wanna go now."

I just laughed. "You wouldn't think it was so much fun if you had to go to school every day of your life, Bobbie. You can go for me if you want to. I'll give you my lunch box and backpack. You'll change your mind."

I saw Dad, Grandpa, Mom, Grandma and Megan go inside a big room, so Bobbie and I ran to catch up with them. The room had two tables full of food and lots of chairs in circles. Bobbie told me she wanted to talk to Mom and Dad. She said she had some questions. What else is new? But Mom and Dad were talking to other people and hugging people they didn't even know. Grandpa and Grandma and Megan were doing it too! I wanted to get away from there so nobody I didn't know would hug me. I don't even like people I know hugging me.

We had to stand in line behind some people and pick up a plate and napkin like they were doing. Then we piled the plate with six kinds of fancy cookies. We got some punch too.

We followed the people to one of the circles of chairs. The people looked nice. They were very old—like Grandpa and Grandma. They sat down and started eating their cake, so Bobbie and I sat down too. I looked around at the people, then I whispered to Bobbie, "You could ask them your questions. They look nice."

She didn't waste a second. "Hi! I'm Bobbie Schmidt. That's my dad over there. He's the one with the wet hair. He got dunked tonight. Do you have a school here? How old do you have to be to go to it? Can I come?" What a sister! She couldn't ask just one question.

The lady smiled though. "Well, honey, I'm glad to meet you. We're Mr. and Mrs. Corbett. Mr. Corbett used to be the pastor here, but now we're retired and just helping out when we can. We do have classes here for children and adults of all ages. If you're alive, we have a class for you! We even have a class for old people like us! We meet on Sunday morning before the big service when everyone gets together in the auditorium."

Mrs. Corbett stopped to take a bite of food. And Bobbie just kept staring at her. I guess she wanted to know more. So Mrs. Corbett swallowed and kept talking. "We also have special classes in the summer when school is out. They're called Vacation Bible School. In fact, they start tomorrow morning. Perhaps your mom would let you come. I could pick you and your brother up and bring you. Don't you also have a sister who played a song on the piano tonight? Megan is her name, if I recall it."

Mrs. Corbett seemed nice enough. She remembered Megan's name. So I answered her, "We do have a sister named Megan. My mom would probably let Bobbie come to summer school at church, but I don't think I would like it. School's hard for me. I don't want to go in the summer! I don't want to do anything that's even a little like school. Besides, I'm pretty old to learn stuff at church." I was trying to be polite.

"Well, young man, you're never too old to learn more about God, and once you know a lot, you're ready to help others learn what you know. I enjoy helping others learn about God. You might change your mind if you knew all that goes on here. We have a Bible story and refreshments and games outside with our youth pastor. There are prizes, and most kids like it even if they don't like school school."

Bobbie got real excited then. "I'll come! I'll come! Do we learn about God too? Do we sing? Do they have big crayons and fat pencils? Does the big-little shepherd come? Please ask my mom if I can come."

I wasn't really excited, but it didn't sound so bad. "Are you sure there are no report cards? They don't do math, do they? I'm really bad at math. Maybe I could come one day and see if I like it. I don't have to go, do I?"

Mrs. Corbett shook her head. "No, son, you don't have to come, but we have hundreds of kids who love it and come back every day and bring friends with them. I promise you there are no report cards, but what you learn is so much more important than anything you could ever learn in school. It will help you all your life—and in the next life too!" Mrs. Corbett made it sound good.

"I don't know much about God or the Bible. But if you're sure there are no report cards, maybe I will give it a try."

Verse to Read

Acts 2:42: "And they continued stedfastly in the apostles' doctrine and fellowship, and in breaking of bread, and in prayers."

QUESTIONS TO ASK YOUR CHILD
1. Will you ever be too old to learn more about God?
2. What should you do after you learn about God?
3. Why is church school so important?

Why Are They Eating in Church?

Megan shouted from the kitchen, "Mom, Topher is going to the living room with his potato chips and soda!"

Toph shouted back. "I am not!"

"You are too! I can see you getting ready to sit down on the couch. You know Mom doesn't want you in there with food. You're sloppy, and you spill stuff, Toph."

"Mind your own business, Megan. I'm going out to the back porch. I was just getting my baseball magazine from the end table."

Megan and Toph argue sometimes. That's what brothers and sisters do. Megan watches everyone. She makes sure no one eats food anywhere in the house except in the kitchen or the dining room.

Later Megan tattled again. "Mom, Bobbie's taking her cereal bowl into the family room to watch cartoons while she eats."

Bobbie tried to whisper. But whenever she whispers, everyone can hear. "Shhhh, Megan! I won't spill it. Don't tell Mom. She'll make me go back to the kitchen, and I'll miss 'Mighty Dog' and 'Super Cat' on TV."

"Megan! Please come here for a minute," Mom called from upstairs. Megan smiled a silly smile at Bobbie and Toph. She thought Mom was going to thank her for telling on the others.

Boy was she surprised at what Mom told her! "Megan, I appreciate your trying to help your brother and sister remember the family rule about eating only in the dining room and kitchen. But I am tired of the tattletale voice you use to tell on the others. Please mind your own business, and I will deal with your brother and sister. Do you understand?"

Megan stopped smiling then and quietly told Mom, "I'm sorry."

In the car on the way to church the next Sunday, Mom gave a speech about not chewing gum in church. "It isn't polite to chew gum in church. This is the place to worship God, and smacking on gum just isn't proper behavior. I want all of you to spit out your gum in the rest room before the service."

Toph didn't like that rule. "But, Mom! This is a new stick of gum, and I don't have any more left. Can't I just hold it still in my mouth?"

Mom didn't go for that idea. "No, Topher, I want it out of your mouth. Do you have the wrapper? Maybe we could save it that way till after church."

They got to church a little late, so they sat in the next-to-the-back row. Bobbie sat next to Dad in case she had a question. He was the best at answering them. "Dad, why is there a white sheet on that table up front by Pastor? Is someone sleeping under there? He'll wake up and see everyone watching him!" Bobbie giggled. She was thinking about that person waking up in his pajamas in front of the church.

But Dad explained: "No, honey, that's the communion table covering. The sheet is covering trays of bread and tiny cups of juice for a special service later."

"Are people going to eat in church? Mom won't even let us chew gum. What will God think? I thought we weren't supposed to eat in church!" Bobbie was afraid to do something wrong.

"Oh, it's OK. We're supposed to be having this meal in church, Bobbie. When Jesus had His last meal with His disciples, He told them to do this often to remember what happened to Him that night and the next few days. When the church was begun, people met in homes, and it was natural to eat together. Now we meet in bigger buildings, and it does seem a little different to have food here."

Bobbie seemed to understand what Dad was saying since she thought of new questions. "What happened to Jesus that next few days? Was it fun? Was it good?"

Dad was glad they were sitting in the back so he could explain to Bobbie about the Lord's Table, or communion. "Well actually, after that special dinner with His friends, Jesus went to court, and the judge found Him guilty. Then He was killed. He hurt a whole lot. He bled and died on the cross for our sins. Then another friend who was rich and some ladies who loved Him a lot got permission to bury Him."

"I don't want to remember that! It sounds very sad!"

"Bobbie, it was necessary. And Jesus didn't stay dead. In three days He came back alive again! That was the happy day! But if He didn't die, our sins couldn't be forgiven. Jesus was the only One Who could take the punishment for us. It was a sad but happy day when Jesus died for our sins and took them away."

"Oh." Bobbie stared at the food for a second. "Can I eat in church, too, Dad?"

"Bobbie, first you need to trust Jesus as your Savior, and then you should be baptized like I was. Eating this meal is only for people in the family of God. It's a special time to remember what Jesus did for you. Mom and I are going to eat today. You watch, and we can talk more at home. But, Bobbie, you may hold my bread and juice until I need to eat them."

Bobbie took the bread from Dad and smiled at him. "Someday I'll eat in church too," she whispered.

Verses to Read

1 Corinthians 11:23–29

This passage describes a service in which the Lord's Supper is observed.

QUESTIONS TO ASK YOUR CHILD

1. What happened to Jesus after the special dinner with His friends?
2. Why do people eat bread and drink juice in church?
3. What do you have to do before you can eat the special meal at church?

Who Helps the Shepherd?

Right before school started again, I got to go on my most awesome adventure ever. I did it all by myself! I flew on an airplane for my first time ever. And I spent two weeks at Grandpa and Grandma Williams' farm—all by myself.

Being on the plane was great! A flight attendant fastened my seat belt. While I waited for the plane to take off, I looked in the pocket in front of me. I found a magazine with pictures in it.

When the plane took off, I felt a little sick in my stomach, but I chewed some gum Mom had given me. At first, I chewed so hard I thought my jaw would crack in two.

Finally we were off the ground. The roads looked like pretend roads that I build in the sandbox. And the houses looked like the little buildings on my miniature railroad. The cars and trucks looked like the cars I use on my roadway cloth.

At first I was a little scared. But then it was fun. It didn't last very long though. I didn't really want it to end, but I was excited about seeing Grandpa and Grandma. The pilot told us to buckle our seat belts again because the plane was getting ready to land. When I looked out the window, I could see things that looked like my railroad and roadway cloth again.

Grandma and Grandpa were at the airport to meet me, and they got my suitcase off the conveyor belt. I learned that word "conveyor belt" from the lady standing next to us at the airport. She was waiting for her suitcases too.

The reason I got to fly to Pennsylvania was so I could help Grandpa with the sheep for the rest of the summer. Grandpa's knees were bothering him.

The next morning, before the sun was even up, Grandpa came into my room. "Rise and shine, young man. There's work to be done!" Grandpa's always cheerful in the morning. I was still sleeping and dreaming about my plane ride to Pennsylvania. I didn't want to get up at first.

But by the time I got dressed and went to the kitchen to eat, I was excited! "How many sheep are there, Grandpa? Where do we start? What can I do to help?"

"You're sounding like your little sister with so many questions, young man!" Grandpa teased me. "I had 60 sheep last year and then 20 more lambs born this spring, so that makes 80 altogether. Fill that jug with water from the hose, and we'll haul water out to the fields for the young ones. I'm so glad to have help. This work is getting to be too much for me. Thanks for coming to help, son."

Mom and Dad called that night. They talked to me first and then to Grandpa and Grandma. Then they let me talk to Bobbie and Megan. "Bobbie, it's awesome! We hauled water to the sheep. The baby lambs are so cute. I chased down two sheep that needed to see the vet and got them into the little trailer for Grandpa. We went swimming in the lake, and tonight we're going for ice cream. Next week is another fair, and I get to help show the animals. Grandpa is hoping to get a good price for them. Grandpa calls me his little shepherd. I miss you." I was hurrying to tell her everything I could think of.

I'm afraid I got Bobbie confused. "You're Grandpa's little shepherd, Toph? Is Grandpa the big shepherd? Do you stand in front of the sheep and hold a big book?" Bobbie was mixing things up with what Mom and Dad had told her about the pastor at church.

"No, Bobbie, you're all confused. I'm the shepherd's helper. I don't talk to the sheep. I feed them water and grain, and I help the sick ones. I'm Grandpa's extra pair of knees since his knees aren't feeling very strong. The doctor says he shouldn't work so hard anymore. Grandpa calls me his deacon. I'm not sure what that means, but maybe Dad knows. I gotta go now."

Bobbie gave the phone to Megan so she could talk to me. Then I guess Bobbie asked Dad, "What's a deacon? Why does Grandpa call Topher a deacon? Do deacons take care of the sheep?"

"Well, the Bible says a deacon is a man who helps the pastor take care of the sheep in the church. Actually a deacon is a pastor's helper who does things to help the people in the church grow and love God more. Grandpa is teasing because Topher is really just helping with the animals, but Grandpa is comparing Topher to a special helper in the church."

Those two weeks were the best two weeks of my life! I learned tons about sheep: how to know if they're sick, what to do if they're sick, how to help them get better, what they eat, how to rescue them when they get caught in the fence or escape to a neighbor's field. And maybe some day I'll be a deacon in the church. I liked taking care of sheep.

Verses to Read

1 Timothy 3:8–10, 12: "Likewise must the deacons be grave, not doubletongued, not given to much wine, not greedy of filthy lucre [getting money dishonestly]; holding the mystery of the faith in a pure conscience. And let these also first be proved; then let them use the office of a deacon, being found blameless. . . . Let the deacons be the husbands of one wife, ruling their children and their own houses well."

QUESTIONS TO ASK YOUR CHILD

1. What is a deacon?
2. How does a deacon help a pastor?

Why Do They Pass the Fancy Frisbees?

One day after Toph got back from his trip to Grandpa and Grandma's, he and Bobbie picked up empty soda cans from the side of the road. They asked Megan to come too, but she was practicing her next song for church. Picking up cans is a great thing! Bobbie and Toph cleaned the road and got some money from recycling the cans. But most of all, they got out of the house when Megan was going to practice her song a hundred times.

Bobbie carried the trash bag, and Toph picked up the cans and threw them in. They made a pretty good team and had fun too. "Seventy-five, seventy-six, seventy-seven." Toph counted every can they put in the bag.

Later on, Dad took Bobbie and Toph to the recycling place to get their money. All together they had collected 150 cans. That would be 50 cents for each of them. Bobbie asked the recycling lady to give her the money in nickels so she could have more money. Toph got five dimes. Since his money was smaller, Bobbie thought she had more money than Toph.

On Sunday Toph put his money in his pants pocket. The money sounded great when it rubbed together. He wanted to spend his 50 cents on baseball cards next Saturday when Mom went shopping. That's the only time Toph likes to go shopping with Mom—when he has money for cards or when they go to the mall in Eastman.

Bobbie put her money in the purse Megan had given her for her birthday. Bobbie liked the sound her nickels made when they bumped each other.

The Schmidts had been going to Sunday School and church every week for a while. Bobbie loved going to "church school." That's what she called it. Megan and Toph liked it more all the time. After Sunday School they went to the auditorium and sat with Mom and Dad. After they had sung a song, Bobbie noticed the Pastor give some men four shiny silver plates. After Pastor prayed, Bobbie asked, "What are those shiny Frisbees, Dad?" Bobbie had never noticed them before.

Dad told her that they're offering plates. "The ushers pass them around so people can give a gift to God. Here come the ushers now."

Mom tapped Bobbie on the leg and asked, "Bobbie, do you and Topher have your money with you?" Bobbie got her money out of her purse and showed Mom. Then Mom told her, "Trade Topher two of your nickels for one of his dimes, please." Mom was whispering so the people around the family wouldn't hear her and look at them the way they did sometimes when Bobbie asked a question.

Bobbie didn't seem to like Mom's idea. "But, Mom, then Topher will have more money than I do!" She didn't really understand money. She thought that the bigger money was better.

Mom just whispered back, "Don't argue with me, Bobbie. It's fair. I'll tell you about it later. When the offering plate comes by, Topher and Bobbie, both of you put one nickel in."

"But, Mom, it's my money. Who gets it if I put it in the Frisbee?"

Mom tried to explain a little. "It's for Pastor and to buy papers and crayons for your Sunday School class. Hurry with your money, or the offering will pass you by."

Bobbie started to pout. "Why can't Pastor make his own money? Why does he have to have mine? I'm poor." People were looking and smiling. They could hear everything Bobbie said.

Mom gave up and decided to wait to explain it. "Never mind, Bobbie," she said. "I'll talk to you later. Please be quiet."

At home Mom told Bobbie, Megan and Toph about sharing part of what you have with God as a gift. "Giving is a way of telling God how much you love Him."

"Could I just tell God I love Him and keep my money?" Bobbie really liked her money.

"Actually, Bobbie, everything you have belongs to God. What if He decided to tell you He loved you and never gave you anything? You would have no air to breathe, no grass to play in, no bed to sleep in, no mom or dad. And certainly no money of your own."

"Everything belongs to God? Oh—" Bobbie was quiet for a little bit. Then she finally said, "OK. How much do I have to give Him?"

"You don't have to give Him anything, but in Bible times people usually gave God one penny out of every ten pennies that they had. I want you to think about how much you love God and how much money you would like to give next Sunday in the offering."

Verses to Read

1 Corinthians 16:1–3: "Now concerning the collection for the saints, as I have given order to the churches of Galatia, even so do ye. Upon the first day of the week let every one of you lay by him in store, as God hath prospered him, that there be no gatherings when I come. And when I come, whomsoever ye shall approve by your letters, them will I send to bring your liberality unto Jerusalem."

The Bible mentions a generous church that was willing to give to the needs of the poorer saints in Jerusalem. Read more about it in 1 Corinthians 16:1–3, where Paul gives instructions about when to give, how often and with what attitude.

QUESTIONS TO ASK YOUR CHILD

1. Why do churches have offering plates?
2. What is the money used for?
3. How much should you give to God?

8

I Have a Question About the
FUTURE

Hints and Helps

Do you like to know what is ahead as you travel down a road? Signs help adults, but children, whether they can read or not, often ignore signs and prefer another method of finding out what they want to know. When kids are young, they ask the universal question, "Are we there yet?" And parents give the universal answer, "Not yet; be patient." But young children cannot read signs, and they don't know where they are.

Even adults want to know where they are going—figuratively as well as literally. Chicago has a special financial institution called the futures market. New York City is home of the New York Stock Exchange, the stock market where people buy and sell shares in various companies. They buy and sell based on a company's present condition and on their own judgment about the company's future. We are all interested in the future.

At every age throughout childhood, we wished that we were older and that the future would arrive more quickly. When we were in kindergarten, we longed for first grade. When we were in junior high, we could not wait until high school. And when we were in high school, we longed for graduation.

The Bible has a lot to say about the future. A number of Bible books reveal a great deal about the future. Important ones are Daniel, Isaiah and Revelation, although we can find many other Bible references concerning the future. Jesus talked a lot about the future. He told His disciples that He was going to Heaven to prepare a place for them so that when they died, they could be with Him.

Each of us has a body, which is the outer man, and a soul and spirit, which is the inner man. At death, a Christian's physical body goes into the grave, but the inner man goes to Heaven (2 Corinthians 5:6–8). At the Resurrection, the Christian's body will resurrect and will go to Heaven to be reunited with the inner man. At that same time the living saints will be raptured, or taken up, by transformation without death (1 Thessalonians 4:13–18).

The Bible reveals much more about the future, but we should note one of the important facts: the Bible teaches that Christ will someday rule over everyone and everything with His Father in Heaven (1 John 3:1–3; Revelation 22:12–17).

What Happens to People When They Die?

"I get the window!" I called that to Megan and Bobbie as they got into the car. I still had to finish packing my backpack for the trip to Trent's in Atlanta.

But when I got to the car, Megan was sitting by one window, and Bobbie had taken the other one. I asked Bobbie to move to the middle so I could get in the car. She wouldn't move. I started to make her move, but Mom came out then.

"Children, you'll have to take turns. Topher, let the girls take the windows until we stop next time for gasoline. Then you can trade with one of them. Does that sound fair?" Mom always tries to find a solution that makes everyone happy.

This time I mumbled, "Sure." Then I had to crawl over Bobbie to get to my seat.

Just after we got out of town, Mom said she had an idea. She was really trying to keep everyone happy. "Why don't we play the cow game? You count all the cows or horses on your side of the road. The first one to 100 wins. If you pass a cemetery, you lose all your points and have to start over again. Everybody understand the rules?"

I looked out Bobbie's window, since I could see over her head. "I got ten over there in that pasture." I was the first one to score.

"I have seven here." Megan scored next.

"I don't have any! I can't play because there are no more sides of the road." I think Bobbie was feeling sorry for herself because I beat her in counting the cows. She's only four, and she can't count very fast.

Mom tried to make her feel better. "Don't give up easily, Bobbie. Keep your eyes open, and you'll score soon. How about if we changed the game and you get to count sheep on both sides of the road? What do you think?" Mom was full of ideas.

"Uh-huh. That's a good idea." Bobbie was happier after that.

"Eighty-eight, eighty-nine, ninety! I'm going to win." I was way ahead of the others.

Just then Megan spotted a cemetery on my side of the road. "See that cemetery by the little church up there on the hill? Ha! You lose all your points."

"I don't see it. You made that up, Megan. I have 95 points now." I did think maybe I saw a cemetery, but I wasn't going to tell Megan I did. She would have won.

Mom solved the problem again. "I did see the cemetery, Topher. And, Megan, you lose ten points for pointing out someone else's cemetery. Watch on your own side of the road."

Bobbie had a question. "What's a cemetery? And how come it makes

Topher lose all his points?" Even with looking out both windows, Bobbie wasn't getting many points. But she was thinking of lots of questions.

I could answer that one. "A cemetery is for dead people, Bobbie. It's where you put the bodies after people quit breathing. It's like bad luck. That's why you lose all your points."

Bobbie looked a little scared. "When I fell off my tricycle last week, I quit breathing, and you didn't put me into a cemetery."

237

Mom had to help me explain better. "Cemeteries are for people whose hearts have stopped beating and who have stopped breathing forever. There is no life left in them. It's what happened to Grandma Jenkins from church last week. She was very old. Her heart quit, and she stopped breathing."

Then we got more questions. "Do people stay there for long? Does it hurt to be in a cemetery? Why do they have those stones? I don't want to be in a cemetery. It sounds really yucky."

Mom had more answers. "It's only your body that is buried in the cemetery. You can't feel anything when you're dead. Your body is there, but the real you inside goes to Heaven if you love Jesus. The stone is there so that people can know where each person is buried. Someday when Jesus comes back, each body will be rejoined with its person and live in Heaven forever—if that person loves Jesus."

Megan stopped counting cows for a second and said, "Then a cemetery isn't bad luck. If you love Jesus, it's a place for your body to wait for Him."

"Cemeteries are nice. I think we should get ten extra points when we see a cemetery!" And for once Bobbie had a really good idea.

Verse to Read

Hebrews 9:27: "And as it is appointed unto men once to die, but after this the judgment."

QUESTIONS TO ASK YOUR CHILD

1. What is buried in a cemetery?
2. What happens to a person who loves Jesus when he dies?
3. When Jesus comes back, what will happen to those who have died and loved Jesus?

Is This Everybody in Jesus?

"Mom, will you show me these pictures?" Bobbie had been in the basement. She came upstairs with a photo album from when Mom was a girl. "Who are these people? Do you know them?"

Mom stopped doing the dishes. "Come over to the couch and sit down with me, Bobbie. I haven't seen this album for a long time." She opened the book. "Oh my, that's Aunt Ruth. She was a dear women who really loved God. Here is Uncle Clyde. He was killed in a car accident when I was just a little girl. My mom told me that Uncle Clyde loved Jesus when he was a boy and made a decision at camp to become a Christian."

"Where is Uncle Clyde now, Mom? Is he with Jesus in Heaven?" That was an important question. Sometimes Bobbie does ask big things.

Mom nodded. "Yes, Bobbie. I believe Uncle Clyde is with Jesus. My mom had a very large family, and each of them loved the Lord. Most of them aren't alive anymore."

Bobbie stared at the picture of Uncle Clyde. Her nose almost touched the page. "Did you ever have all your family together? Does God ever get all of His family together and have a family renoonon like we had in Texas last year for Dad's family?"

"That's 'reunion,' honey." Mom hugged Bobbie. "I love you, Bobbie. I love your questions. You often ask the most important questions of the day! Now let's see about answers. I have never met Aunt Ginny, Uncle Jim or Grandma VanAllen. They were all with Jesus before I was born. I know them from pictures, but not face-to-face. We try to get together as often as we can, but we're such a large family it's hard with all the work schedules. And now our family has moved around and lives farther apart. I have cousins from California to Vermont, Wisconsin to Texas. What else did you ask?" Mom tried to remember, but Bobbie had asked so many questions at the same time.

"Does God ever get all His family together? He must have tons of aunts and uncles. . . ."

"Bobbie, God has children only, no grandchildren and no aunts or uncles. No one else lived before God, so no one in the world is older or smarter than He is. But He does have many sons and daughters, people who have accepted the free gift of payment for sin that Jesus provided when He died on the cross."

"OK. Just sons and daughters. So do they ever get all together for a renoo—"

"Reunion." Mom and Bobbie said it slowly together.

"Well, like my family, some have already died and gone to Heaven to be with Jesus forever. Many are still alive, but they live all around the world. Everywhere that people live, God has some sons and daughters. The Bible says God is building a family from every tribe and tongue and nation under the sun. God has others who will be in His family who are not even born yet."

"How does He build a family from tongues, Mom?" Bobbie took it just like it sounded. But Mom didn't really mean building from tongues.

Mom tried to explain it. "It means people from every different language spoken on earth. It really means people from everywhere."

"So why doesn't it say that? Why do they make it hard?" Bobbie was quiet for a little bit. She thought about the people from everywhere trying to get

together for a reunion. Then she asked, "So for some people, it would be too far to travel to a reunion?"

Mom nodded again. "Yes, but someday Jesus is coming back in the clouds to give everybody a free ride to Heaven so that He can have all His family together. It will be better than being an astronaut or a jet pilot. The Bible says that those who died loving Jesus will go to the reunion first, then those who are still alive on the earth will go next. And all of us who love Jesus will meet Him in the air. We will get to be with Him forever."

"How will we get there? in planes? big balloons? rockets?"

"We'll get there without any kind of traveling machine. Jesus will just take those who love Him. We will just go up in the air—"

Bobbie started jumping up and down, over and over. Mom asked her, "What are you doing?"

Bobbie looked at Mom like Mom was supposed to know what Bobbie was doing. "Mom! I'm getting ready for the reunion."

Verses to Read

John 17:20–23: "Neither pray I for these alone, but for them also who shall believe on me through their word; that they all may be one; as thou, Father, art in me, and I in thee, that they also may be one in us: that the world may believe that thou hast sent me. And the glory which thou gavest me I have given them; that they may be one, even as we are one: I in them, and thou in me, that they may be made perfect in one. . . ."

This is the prayer that Jesus prayed for those who are in His family—past, present and future. For a description of the reunion in the sky, read 1 Thessalonians 4:13–18.

QUESTIONS TO ASK YOUR CHILD

1. What kind of family does God have?
2. When will all of God's family be together?
3. Are you a part of God's family?

What If You Miss the Family Reunion?

"I'll name the player, and you tell me what basketball team he played for. OK, Bobbie?"

"Topher, I don't like this game. It's too hard. Can't we do something else?" Bobbie doesn't like it when Toph pretends she is his little brother. But he wants her to know all the important basketball facts. That way when his friends come over, he can show them how smart his little sister is.

He practically had to beg her. "Please, Bobbie! You're getting so good. We won't do too many this time. I promise."

Finally she gave in. "OK, only because I love you, Toph! Make the first ones easy."

"Shaquielle O'Neal?"

"Orlando Magic."

"Right! Bobbie, good guess! How about Scottie Pippen?"

"He's for the Chicago Bullets."

Toph smiled a little. But he didn't laugh, or she would have stopped playing. "No, it's the Chicago Bulls, Bobbie. But you were close. All right, little sister. Charles Barkley?"

"Phoenix Sunrays?"

Toph just smiled again. "Close! Phoenix Suns. How about Isiah Thomas?"

"He plays for Detroit Pistons."

"Yes! OK, here's a hard one—Michael Jordan played for _____?"

"Chicago Bulls! Ha! I got it! Now let's play my game. I learned it at Sunday School, and I kind of made it up. I'll say a person in the Bible, and you tell me if he's in God's family or not. Ready?"

"Oh Bobbie, I learn some stuff in Sunday School and children's church, but Mom's been reading the Bible to you since your birthday. You pro'bly know more than I do. Go easy on me, OK?"

"How about Moses? In God's family, or not?"

"Yes. He was God's leader in the Old times."

"It's Old Testament." Bobbie was so pleased to know about the Bible. "You were close. How about Goliath?"

Toph just had to think for a second. "He's a bad guy, I think. I'll say he's not in the family of God."

Bobbie patted him on the back. "Good job, Topher. He was a bad giant. How about Hannah?"

Toph didn't even try to think about that one. "Hannah? I've never heard of him. Who's he?"

"It's a girl! She was Samuel's mother. She's in God's family. How about Mr. Schmidt?"

"That one I know for sure. In the family!"

"OK. Megan Schmidt? and Topher Schmidt?"

Toph wasn't sure what to say about Megan. "We should ask Megan. But I'm sure about me! I believed on Jesus and got into God's family at Grandpa and Grandma's house last summer. I'm glad I'm in God's family. Last week in church school I learned that when Jesus comes back to take the people in His family to Heaven with Him, everyone else will get left behind. Then they're going to have a terrible time of trouble. They won't be able to find food to eat, and the bad guys will be in charge of everything!" Then Toph thought of something kind of sad and scary. He wasn't sure if Bobbie was in God's family or not. "I want you to come with us, Bobbie!"

"I want to come too, Toph. Let's go talk to Mom. I want to be in God's family too."

Verses to Read

John 3:36: "He that believeth on the Son hath everlasting life: and he that believeth not the Son shall not see life; but the wrath of God abideth on him."

Matthew 24:21: "For then shall be great tribulation, such as was not since the beginning of the world to this time, no, nor ever shall be."

QUESTIONS TO ASK YOUR CHILD

1. When Jesus comes back, what happens to those who don't love Him?
2. Will you go with Jesus, or will you be left behind?

Where Will the
Reunion Meet?

I know the Cleveland Browns aren't the greatest team. But we live near Cleveland, and everybody there loves the Browns. It doesn't matter if the Browns are good or bad or just OK; we love the Browns. This fall I had my next-best most awesome adventure. Dad and I went to a real National Football League game! We got to see the Browns play up close!

When Dad and I were getting ready to leave, Mom was fussing over me as if I were a little kid and not almost nine years old. "Here, put on another shirt. And carry these two sweatshirts. I know best, and the more layers you have on, the warmer you'll be. It's supposed to be in the 30s today at the stadium. Don't forget your hooded sweatshirt. You'll be glad you have it."

Finally Dad and I got in the car and left. I asked questions the whole way. I think it was because I was so excited. Dad laughed and said I sounded like Bobbie. Yuck!

After we parked our car and walked to the stadium, I hardly said anything. I had never seen so many people at the same time. I was kind of afraid a few times because I thought I couldn't see Dad. I was afraid I'd get lost and never be found, so I stayed as close to Dad as I could. I felt a lot better when we found our seats and sat down.

The game was a close one. Dad and I cheered until we couldn't even talk. We lost our voices. It was a good thing we cheered so hard, because it helped the Browns to win. That was a great day for football!

On our way home, I got to wondering about all those people. I asked Dad, "When we get to Heaven, will there be as many people as there were at the game today?"

"Topher, that's a great question. Maybe Bobbie's rubbing off on you." Dad laughed. And I laughed too. It was funny. Then Dad answered me. "There'll be too many people in Heaven to count. But it will seem like lots of people. Today's game had an all-time record attendance of 60,000. That's nothing compared with Heaven. There will be people from as far back as Adam and Eve through the Old times and the New times and people alive today and some not yet born. It will be quite a crowd. I'm sure glad that you made certain last summer that you will be with them, Toph!"

"So am I, Dad. Where will we meet that will hold that many people? Does God have a huge stadium or something for us all to meet in?"

Dad smiled. "Well, I've learned from the Bible that Jesus has gone to Heaven to get a place ready for all of us who love Him. It must be a very big place, because He made the earth in seven days, and He's been in Heaven getting this place ready for more than 2,000 years! In John, chapter 14, Jesus described the place as 'mansions.' I can't wait to see what He has ready. I've always wanted to live in a mansion. How about you, Topher?"

I did think that sounded good.

Verses to Read

    John 14:2, 3: "In my Father's house are many mansions: if it were not so, I would have told you. I go to prepare a place for you. And if I go and prepare a place for you, I will come again, and receive you unto myself; that where I am, there ye may be also."

QUESTIONS TO ASK YOUR CHILD
1. What is Jesus doing in Heaven?
2. The Bible says the place will be like what?
3. Will you have a mansion in Heaven?

How Long Will
We Be There?

"Do we have to go to the dentist today, Mom?" Megan was scared and hoped Mom would say no.

"Sorry, honey, but we're going after lunch."

"How long will we be there? I hope not long enough for me to have a turn."

Mom patted Megan on the back to help her not be scared. "Sorry, but each of you children is scheduled for a checkup today. You had better get into the bathroom to brush your teeth. I'll set the timer. I want you to brush your teeth until it goes off. Then rinse your mouth really well." Mom knows how much

Megan doesn't like going to the dentist.

A few days later Toph asked Mom if they were going to the state fair this year. "I loved it when we went to the fair at Grandma and Grandpa's. We are going, aren't we?"

"Topher, we were planning to go, but now I don't know if we'll be able to go to the fair or not. Dad has to work overtime on a construction project. We may not be able to go after all."

That was the worst news Toph had heard forever. "Mom, that's terrible! Can I go with Tommy's family if we don't go? They'd let me if you asked them. Please? Please? You know that I love the fair."

Mom didn't answer right away. It's hard when she makes him wait. She told him, "We'll have to talk with Dad, Topher. I would like for you to be able to go, but we'll have to see."

"Does that mean yes? It means yes, doesn't it, Mom!" Toph kept bugging her because he really wanted to go to the state fair.

"Be patient, Topher. Your dad and I will talk about it tonight. We'll let you know as soon as we can."

When it was still summer, Bobbie asked Mom, "When will I get to start school? How long will I get to be there?"

Mom told her to be patient too. "Bobbie, you're still too young to go to school all day. When school starts in a few weeks, you'll go to kindergarten. You'll go in the mornings and come home right before lunch, just like in preschool." Bobbie had been asking to go to school since she was really little. She went to preschool last year, and she loved it. Now she didn't want to wait even a few more weeks for kindergarten to start.

"But, Mom, you said I could go to school pretty soon. I can't wait any longer. I want to go now. I want to stay forever. I love school. Why can't you call and tell them that I'm coming? It's been forever already, Mom. I can't wait anymore." Bobbie used her most whiny voice.

Mom told her, "Bobbie, you'll have to wait whether you want to or not. And forever is a very long time. It never ends. Do you want to sleep at school and never come home for dinner? We sure will miss you here."

Bobbie thought for a little bit. Soon she said, "No, I guess I don't want to be at school forever. I love you and Dad and Topher and Megan." Then she ran up to her room. In a few minutes she came back downstairs. She had more questions. "Mom, how long will we be in Heaven? Is that forever too? Won't we ever come back home for dinner or to see Shep? Who will cut our grass while we're gone?"

"Heaven is forever. And it's going to be wonderful, Bobbie! You won't want to come back here for anything. God will take care of all of our needs. He'll feed us and give us a place to stay. I am so glad that our whole family will be there. Forever will not seem long because we will be with the One we love—Jesus! That's the best part about Heaven—Jesus is going to be there!"

Verse to Read

1 Thessalonians 4:17: "Then we which are alive and remain shall be caught up together with them in the clouds to meet the Lord in the air: and so shall we ever be with the Lord."

QUESTIONS TO ASK YOUR CHILD

1. How long will saved people be in Heaven?
2. What is the best thing about Heaven?
3. Are you going to Heaven?

What Will We Do in Heaven?

Megan was on the phone with her friend Kendra. They were talking about camp.

"What will we do at Camp Cayuga?" Megan asked her. "Is it like church all day for a week? I don't think I could take that much church. Have you been there before, Kendra? Is it fun? How much does it cost?"

Mom and Bobbie were baking cookies in the kitchen when Megan got off the phone. "Mom, Kendra wants to know if I can go to Camp Cayuga with her next week. Can I go?"

"What will you do there, Megan? Are there counselors? Who's the speaker? How will you get there? How much does it cost?" Mom sure asked a lot of questions.

"Mom, you sound like Bobbie! Kendra says that she had a super counselor last summer. There's one meeting in the morning and one at night. They have time for crafts, swimming, hiking, horseback riding. There's a snack place where you can get candy and ice cream and pop. I don't know how we get there. Kendra didn't know the cost. Maybe you could call Kendra's mom and ask your other questions. I think I really want to go. So can I? Can I?"

"It sounds interesting, Megan, but I'll need more information, and I would like to talk it over with your dad before making a decision. Would you please get Mrs. Battalgia's phone number for me? I'll call and talk to her."

Mom went to call Kendra's mom. That's when Bobbie started asking Megan questions. She'd been licking the beaters, and she hadn't been listening to everything Megan had told Mom. "Where's Camp Cay—Cayu—Camp? And what do you do there?" Bobbie asked.

Megan told her, "I think it's in the hilly part of Ohio. You do lots of fun stuff there."

"Can I go? Is it like church all day? Do you sit and listen to the little shepherd talk all the time? Do you want to go, Megan? Is camp like Heaven? Do you play on harps all day? I can't even play a harp. Maybe the angels play the harps and we just hum."

Megan and Toph laughed. They were imagining all the kids at camp wearing wings and playing harps.

When Megan stopped laughing, she answered Bobbie, "I don't know about Heaven, but camp is a lot of fun. You swim, play games, ride horses and eat junk food. Kendra's been there, and she liked it. I think I'll like it too. Ask Mom about Heaven. I don't know what we'll do there. Hope it isn't boring 'cause we're going to be there forever, Mom says." Then Megan started talking about what she wanted to take to camp with her and how much money she could spend at the snack shack.

When Mom got off the phone, Bobbie did ask her Heaven question. "Mom, what will we do in Heaven? Will we hum while the angels play harps?" Bobbie had forgotten about camp since she couldn't go anyway. She did plan to go to Heaven someday though.

"We'll tell God how much we love Him. We'll sing. I think you'll get to sit on Jesus' lap and have Him tell you how much He loves you. We'll get to talk with people from the Bible and make friends with Moses, David, Daniel, Mary, Hannah and Rahab and many others. We'll never get tired of it. God will see to that. We'll sing to Jesus that He is a wonderful Lamb. We won't cry there or be sad or ever go to the doctor or dentist again. We won't have night-lights, because it will always be light there, because Jesus is the light. Grandpa won't need his cane anymore, because his knees won't hurt then."

"There's going to be music though, right? Maybe in Heaven God can make me a perfect piano player. I could be like Megan except never have to practice."

Verses to Read

   Revelation 21:1–4

   These verses tell about the new heaven and the new earth.

QUESTIONS TO ASK YOUR CHILD

1. Name some things that will happen in Heaven?
2. What will not happen in Heaven?
3. Who is the light in Heaven?

Who Goes to Heaven?

"Mom, Cassidy says that I can't go to Heaven because I'm a liar. Will I get to go to Heaven? I really want to."

Bobbie was crying and asking questions at the same time.

"What did you say, Bobbie? What made her think that you are a liar?"

Bobbie sniffed. "I said I wasn't going to camp because I didn't want to go. But Cassidy knows I'm not old enough."

"Well, Bobbie, it's always best to tell the truth. Did you tell her you were sorry? Did you tell her you know you're too young?"

Bobbie nodded and sniffed again. "I did, Mom, but she kept saying I'm a liar and can't go to Heaven. I'm scared, Mom. I want to go to Heaven. Won't Jesus forgive me if I say I'm sorry?"

Bobbie talks about Heaven a lot. She knows that it's wonderful, that Jesus is there, that it's like a big family reunion. She knows that people who love God from as far back as Adam and all the way till now—and people not even born yet—will be there. She knows that Jesus will come in the clouds to get His special people from the cemeteries and get the ones living at that moment too. She knows that those who aren't in God's family when Jesus takes the others will stay here on earth for a time of big trouble. Toph told her that last part.

But Bobbie wasn't sure what happens when a little girl—or someone else—does wrong things after she has asked Jesus to save her.

So she asked Mom if a little girl needs to get saved again. "What happens if someone disobeys God after God puts him into His family? Does the person still get to go to Heaven?"

Mom got out her Bible. "Bobbie, let's check this problem out. Here, I'll read to you from the book of Revelation, where the Bible tells us about those who don't get to go to Heaven." She read the verses. Then she had to explain them to Bobbie. They were kind of hard verses. "It says that murderers will not get to be in Heaven. And people who aren't faithful to their husbands or wives will not get to be in Heaven. And people who worship other gods and worship other things more than God will not get to be in Heaven. And people who get information about the future from worshiping Satan will not get to be in Heaven. It says that liars will not go to Heaven."

She looked down at the Bible again. "It's interesting that it also says that those who are fearful and unbelieving will find out that they, too, will not be in Heaven. I believe that it means people who lie on purpose and live all the time in those sins will not be let into Heaven. The Bible says that Satan is a liar and the father of all lies, so those who lie all the time will not be allowed to enter God's Heaven."

Then Bobbie looked real scared. "But Mom, I want to go to Heaven. I don't lie all the time. I asked for Jesus to forgive me. You said He would. Is that true?"

"Yes, Bobbie, it is true. Those who ask to be forgiven and are genuinely sorry for their sins will be forgiven. God promises to forgive any and all who will admit that they are wrong. The Bible promises that He will forgive every time we ask Him to. It also says that it is fair and right for Him to do so. He wipes your record clean and makes it like you never even did it. Your part is to admit that what you said or did or thought is wrong in God's eyes."

"That's easy, Mom. I already did that part. I am sorry. I learned my lesson. I'm going to be careful about what I say. I love God. I'm going to live with Him forever!"

Verses to Read

 1 Corinthians 15:3, 4: "For I delivered unto you first of all that which I also received, how that Christ died for our sins according to the scriptures; and that he was buried, and that he rose again the third day according to the scriptures."

 1 John 1:9: "If we confess our sins, he is faithful and just to forgive us our sins, and to cleanse us from all unrighteousness."

 Revelation 21:3, 4: "And I heard a great voice out of heaven saying, Behold, the tabernacle of God is with men, and he will dwell with them, and they shall be his people, and God himself shall be with them, and be their God. And God shall wipe away all tears from their eyes; and there shall be no more death, neither sorrow, nor crying, neither shall there be any more pain: for the former things are passed away."

QUESTIONS TO ASK YOUR CHILD

1. Who will not get to go to Heaven?
2. How can you go to Heaven?
3. When you tell God you are sorry for your sins, what happens?

Farewell to Adult Friend

We trust that you and your child have enjoyed this trip into various Bible passages that in a simple way teach us some of the great things of God. May we urge you to make this a beginning and a challenge to deeper reading and understanding God's special instruction manual, the Bible. We would also urge you to be like the family of new believers in the early church who "received the word with all readiness of mind, and searched the scriptures daily, whether those things were so" (Acts 17:11).

Children are indeed full of questions. We hope that this book has helped you to find answers for them. If you don't know the answer yourself, don't be afraid to ask another believer for assistance. As so often happens in this book and in real life, one question properly answered will bring about half a dozen more that deserve answers as well. Relax and enjoy your child's inquisitiveness, knowing that answers to his or her important questions do exist.

We would like to hear from you to learn some of your child's questions that you struggle to answer. If after searching the Bible and discussing a question with your pastor or Christian friend you are still stumped, please feel free to drop Regular Baptist Press a line asking your question.

Good-bye for now! We hope you enjoyed your trip through the world of the child and basic theology!

—Robert Carl Newman
—Cheryl Fawcett